Lectionary Worship Aids

Series V, Cycle B

Dallas A. Brauninger

CSS Publishing Company, Inc., Lima, Ohio

Copyright © 1999 by
CSS Publishing Company, Inc.
Lima, Ohio

Library of Congress Cataloging-in-Publication Data

Brauninger, Dallas A., 1943-
    Lectionary worship aids. Series V / Dallas Brauninger.
        p.   cm.
    Includes bibliographical references and index.
    Contents: [1] Cycle A.
    ISBN 0-7880-1209-6 (cycle A : alk. paper)
    1. Worship programs. 2. Church year. 3. Common lectionary (1992) I. Title.
BV198.B66   1998
264—dc21   98-2527
                                                                         CIP

This book is available in the following formats, listed by ISBN:
    0-7880-1364-5   Book
    0-7880-1365-3   Disk
    0-7880-1366-1   Sermon Prep

PRINTED IN U.S.A.

In Celebration of LD Dolley

Table Of Contents

Preface

Hymns engage persons in worship ... The beginning hymn catches our attention and binds us together ... Creatively presented, a hymn can charm its way into your congregation. Occasionally, provide the tonic of an old-fashioned, memorized hymn, a comfort whose words and automatic tune need not trouble aging eyes ... Congregations accept new words more readily than they learn new tunes. If yours is shy about trying new tunes, first introduce words set to an appropriate, familiar tune. Find compatible tunes for the meter and spirit of the words by using the tune and metrical indices in your hymnal.

These excerpts from a recent series on hymns in *Emphasis: A Preaching Journal For The Parish Pastor*[1] set the tone for the selection of hymns in this worship resource.

The hymns of the church potentially bind our churches together during these times of new clergy sharings among denominations. Merging of congregations promises to bring together a unique mix of clergy and laity. Pastors bring their own repertoires of hymns to a congregation. The greater variety of people opens the way for new sharings. New hymnals expand the possibilities of the sung word in a new century. New tunes refresh well-known words; new words renew well-known tunes.

The revival of certain classical hymns helps diminish denominational homesickness of parishioners. Can a Methodist thrive long without singing "Here I Am, Lord," an Episcopalian without "Come [Down][Forth], O Love Divine," a Presbyterian without "Amazing Grace," or a member of the United Church of Christ without "Christian, Rise And Act Thy Creed"? Might many of our denominations one day share one hymnal?

Hymns for each worship service are coded from 01B through 67B for easy location in the index of hymns at the end of this volume. While this list includes several representative denominational hymnals and two collections by contemporary hymn writers, it is not exhaustive.

Hymn selection for the three cycles of this series offers as much information as lectionary recommendation. The writer means to integrate the rich heritage of classical hymn texts and tunes spanning the denominations with the introduction of less frequently sung tunes and hymns new to the decade.

In several instances where a hymn may not be readily available, the bold-type, upper case "OR" indicates an alternative hymn selection. The lower case "or" marks an optional tune. Such options lend themselves as "teaching hymns" sung often during a month or season.

Several footnoted suggestions submit additional uses of hymns. For example, a verse of "Come, [O][Thou] Long-Expected Jesus" used as a closing congregational response at the extinguishing of the candles throughout Advent ties together the season. Other connecting hymns periodically serve as congregational calls to worship and prayer responses. Some selections offer a congregation/choir duet of a well-known tune with the familiar words and a refreshed text. The antiphonal singing of a hymn completes other services. For certain times of the year, the writer suggests congregational choice of hymns.

As another goal of this series of lectionary worship aids, the writer has reached toward a conversational, familiar manner of prayer in the calls to worship, collects, and prayers of confession. It is hoped that they minimize the religious cliché and will assist worship leaders in drawing today's worshipers toward closer union with each other and with God.

---

1. See Brauninger's "Hymns In The Worship Environment," The Worship Environment column in *Emphasis: A Preaching Journal For The Parish Pastor*, Volume 26, Numbers 2-6 (July-August, 1996 — May-June, 1997).

First Sunday In Advent

First Lesson: Isaiah 64:1-9
Theme: Coming Forth

Call To Worship

Leader: Come forth, O love divine.
People: Meet us in the crevices between hope and hope.
Leader: Come forth, O holy one.
People: Meet us when we fade like the leaf.
All: Come forth, O love divine.

Collect

In so many ways you come forth to us, you ever-concerned and active Parent. So variously you lead all your children, you who works for those who wait for you, even though we hide from you our shortcomings. Let us come forth to you. Amen.

Prayer Of Confession

After all the energy you spend in creation, ever-creating God, we did not expect you also to walk with us. We did not anticipate your coming forward yourself to help straighten out our messes. We thought we were alone in braving adulthood. You might have left us to go on to other matters. Instead, you are coming forth in the shape of a human being to meet us. So now we make ready to receive you. Through Jesus. Amen.

01B Hymns[1]

"Once In Royal David's City" Tune: IRBY
"Come [Down][Forth], O Love Divine" Tune: DOWN AMPNEY
"Now Bless The God Of Israel"[2] Tune: FOREST GREEN
"We Yearn, O [Christ][God], For Wholeness" Tune: PASSION CHORALE

9

First Sunday In Advent

Second Lesson: 1 Corinthians 1:3-9
Theme: "Grace To You"

Call To Worship
Grace to you, and to you, and to you. Grace and peace from God our Holy Parent and from our Savior Jesus Christ. This is the grace God gives. Come, let us worship God this Advent day and receive our Savior's grace.

Collect
Your grace slips into our lives at Advent, O God, as a renewed sense of generosity. Your generous action toward us in the birth of Christ awakens our own good will and our own helpful spirit toward others. More than the fleeting musical embellishment of a grace note, your grace brings sturdiness to our fragile souls. Amen.

Prayer Of Confession
We worship you, O God, who calls us at Advent beyond world-weariness. We worship you, who draws us at Advent to transcend fears that overtake us. We worship you, who reprieves us from seasons of being lost in life. We confess our need and gratitude for your love, your protection, and your gracious kindness. Through the coming of Jesus. Amen.

01B Hymns[1]
"There's A Song In The Air" Tune: CHRISTMAS SONG
"He Came As Grace" Tune: OBERLIN
"Now Bless The God Of Israel"[2] Tune: FOREST GREEN
"God Of Grace And God Of Glory" Tune: CWM RHONDDA

---

1. As either an introit or as a closing before the benediction, sing the verse of "[O][Oh] Come, O Come, Emmanuel" [Tune: VENI EMMANUEL] that begins: "O come, O Wisdom from on high."

2. Sing verse one of "Now Bless The God Of Israel" after the Old Testament reading. This hymn will be sung each Advent Sunday.

First Sunday In Advent

Gospel: Mark 13:24-37
Theme: A Falling Star?

Call To Worship

Christmas is a laser
piercing through boredom's hours
breaking into the hum of frustration,
cutting through pain.

Christmas is a light beam
waiting,
even as its promise and hope burst forth,
waiting for us.

Collect

You give us time to get ready. You give us time to expect. You give us time to wait. And still, ever-birthing God, you surprise us with the ways you come into our lives. We come to you with hearts grateful for your patience. Amen.

Prayer Of Confession

A falling star? No falling star, this that shines its constant sign, yet as easily missed if we are not ready. Creator of the stars of night, let us prepare to receive your promise and your hope. Amen.

01B Hymns[1]

"We Hail You God's Anointed" Tune: ELLACOMBE
"O How Shall I Receive You" Tune: ST. THEODULPH
"Now Bless The God Of Israel"[2] Tune: FOREST GREEN
"Creator Of The Stars Of Night," "O Lord Of Light, Who Made The Stars," or "O Loving Founder Of The Stars" Tune: CONDITOR ALME

Second Sunday In Advent

First Lesson: Isaiah 40:1-11
Theme: "Here Is Your God"

Call To Worship
Leader: Here is your God. Hear God's comfort in your life:
People: Every valley shall be lifted up.
Leader: Hear the energy of God:
People: Every mountain and hill shall be made low.
Leader: Hear the strength of God:
People: The uneven ground shall become level.
Leader: Hear the persistence of God:
People: The rough places shall become a plain.

Collect
O God of tenderness and compassion, our anxieties melt with Isaiah's comforting words. As the shepherd gathers and carries the lambs close to the heart, so does your love embrace us. As the shepherd gently leads the mother sheep, you also guide us around obstacles so we may lead others in your name. Amen.

Prayer Of Confession
Our power and our might threaten to turn into control, God. Our tenderness and our compassion become packed with worthless emotion. Teach us, O God, to marry strength with gentleness so our actions will show your presence in our lives. Amen.

02B Hymns
"Come, [O][Thou] Long-Expected Jesus" Tune: HYFRYDOL
"Comfort, Comfort, [O][These][Ye] My People" Tune: FREU DICH
   SEHR or PSALM 42
"Now Bless The God Of Israel" Tune: FOREST GREEN

Second Sunday In Advent

Second Lesson: 2 Peter 3:8-15a
Theme: While You Wait

Call To Worship
God is waiting to come to us. We are waiting for God to enter our lives. How shall we live while we wait for the world to change? What can we do? How shall we be? Come, let us worship God as we wait for the new.

Collect
No wonder joy bursts out at Christmas, O God, when you, who waits for us to be ready, meet our readiness to receive you. No wonder peace dazes chaos at Christmas. No wonder hope shows its hardy self. To this we say, Amen.

Prayer Of Confession
How will you find us, O God, when you come into our lives? Will you find us waiting passively, waiting for you to do all the work? Will you find us active waiters, preparing the ground and making ready? Will you find us frittering away costly time? Will you find us at peace? Amen.

02B Hymns
"Lift Up Your Heads, [O][Ye] Mighty Gates" Tune: MACHT HOCH DIE TÜR, MILWAUKEE, or TRURO
"All Earth Is Waiting" Tune: SEDONA or TAULÉ
"In The Bleak Midwinter" Tune: CRANHAM

Second Sunday In Advent

Gospel: Mark 1:1-8
Theme: John

Call To Worship
Who is the voice in your wilderness? How do you prepare the way for Christ to enter your life? What is the message you give others by the way you live? These are the questions we bring to worship this second Sunday in Advent as we prepare for Jesus' birth.

Collect
We come, O God, to hear your voice. Let your voice be a beacon of radar that quiets the channel-flitting restlessness in our souls that keeps us from hearing you and recognizing you in our midst. Amen.

Prayer Of Confession
Guide us, Holy Parent, as we appraise the plethora of daily choices that deluge us. Give us clarity of purpose. Help our hearts to be clean. Give us the courage to find our own voices and then to speak out the words that will make a difference to those we care about. Through our Savior, Jesus. Amen.

02B Hymns
"Of The [Father's Love][Parent's Heart] Begotten" Tune: DIVINUM
    MYSTERIUM
"There's A Voice In The Wilderness" Tune: ASCENSION
"The First Nowell" Tune: THE FIRST NOWELL

Third Sunday In Advent

First Lesson: Isaiah 61:1-4, 8-11
Theme: Covenant And Recompense

Call To Worship

Leader: Sent to bring good news to the oppressed,
People: Sent to bind up the brokenhearted,
Leader: To proclaim liberty to the captives,
People: To release the prisoners,
Leader: To comfort all who mourn,
People: Sent to replace a faint spirit with the mantle of praise.
Leader: These are the messages of Advent.
All: Let us give praise to God.

Collect

The covenant you make, O God, is no flighty promise but a vow to affirm creation forever. The recompense you offer is no quick-burning sugar but substantial food for the soul. Amen.

Prayer Of Confession

We come to you, comforting and compassionate Savior, with the hope of being worthy to receive the covenant you make by sending your long-awaited Son. May all — nations and towns, officials and families, leaders and children — arise with renewed vigor to meet the challenges of our day. In the name of Christ. Amen.

03B Hymns

"Come, [O][Thou] Long-Expected Jesus" Tune: STUTTGART
"Comfort, Comfort [O][These][Ye] My People" Tune: FREU DICH
    SEHR or PSALM 42
"Now Bless The God Of Israel"[1] Tune: FOREST GREEN
"A Child Is Born" Tune: VOM HIMMEL HOCH

Third Sunday In Advent

Second Lesson: 1 Thessalonians 5:16-24
Theme: Hold Fast

Call To Worship

Leader: May the God of peace sanctify you entirely; and may the unity of your spirit and your soul and your body be kept sound and blameless at the coming of our Lord Jesus Christ. Come, let us worship the God of peace.

People: Let us give praise to God.

Collect

Be faithful. Be staunch supporters of the faith. Be firm. Be unwavering. Hold fast to what is good. With the strength and encouragement of these words, O God, we hear again our responsibility in receiving the Christ Child. We affirm wanting to do our part to make ready for the holy birth. Amen.

Prayer Of Confession

In our hearts, O God, we know what is right. In these days of many distractions, we would remain focused on what is just, moral, and honest. Help us to screen our words and actions through the teachings of Jesus. Guide our lives as we try to stay faithful to the good. For the sake of our Savior. Amen.

03B Hymns

"Let All Mortal Flesh Keep Silence" Tune: PICARDY
"Wake, Awake, For Night Is Flying" Tune: WACHET AUF
"O Come, All [Ye][You] Faithful" Tune: ADESTE FIDELES

Third Sunday In Advent

Gospel: John 1:6-8, 19-28
Theme: Who Are You?

Call To Worship
"Who are you?" they asked of John. "What do you say about yourself?" How would you answer these questions were God to ask them of you? In light of the coming birth of Jesus, how would you answer? As we prepare for worship, let us take a few minutes to respond in our hearts. Please turn to your neighbor and give voice to one or two words about yourself.

Collect
We come here, O God, as your people with the special identity of being your children. We come with all our diversity of plans, beliefs, backgrounds, and credentials. We come as yours in expectation of your coming in human form to us. Amen.

Prayer Of Confession
"Who are you?" This question calls us to attention. The list grows from defining ourselves in terms of our relationships to ascribing particular qualities, from listing our accomplishments to decrying our shortfalls. "What do you say about yourself?" stirs both our protective nature and our open, hopeful side. What do you say about us, O God? What are your words spoken through the action of your sending your Son to us? Amen.

03B Hymns
"On [River] Jordan's Bank The Baptist's Cry" Tune: WINCHESTER NEW
"Tell Out, My Soul" Tune: WOODLANDS
"O Little Town Of Bethlehem" Tune: FOREST GREEN or ST. LOUIS

---

1. Sing verse two of "Now Bless The God Of Israel" after the Old Testament reading.

17

Fourth Sunday In Advent

First Lesson: 2 Samuel 7:1-11, 16
Theme: Cedar Or Goat's Hair

Call To Worship

We live not in a land of nomads yet we know about the wandering of the human spirit. Come, all you faithful, and worship our faithful God whose presence brings permanence in transitory times. Come and await together the holy birth.

Collect

God, who is truly with us, we make room for you in pauses between our activities. As we make a point to remember your presence while flitting from car to home, from commuter to work, from meeting to meeting and commotion to commotion, let flickers of prayer light our day. In the name of Jesus. Amen.

Prayer Of Confession

Amid the constant uprooting of change, we yearn for a stable home, O God. In the middle of both wanted and unwelcome transitions, we search for something lasting. Let our sense of your presence in our lives be as crumble-resistant as cedar and our capacity to meet life changes as easily resettled as the goat hair walls of the nomad's tent. Amen.

04B Hymns

"[O][Oh] Come, All [Ye][You] Faithful" Tune: ADESTE FIDELES
"Now Bless The God Of Israel"[1] Tune: FOREST GREEN
"Return, My People" Tune: REPTON
"God [Himself][Is Truly] With Us" Tune: ARNSBERG

Fourth Sunday In Advent

Second Lesson: Romans 16:25-27
Theme: To An Able God

Call To Worship

Leader: Glory be to God who is able
People: To strengthen us with the good news of Jesus' birth.
Leader: Glory be to God who is able
People: To bring about allegiance to our faith.
All: All glory be to you, all wise and able God.

Collect

Gracious God, your coming makes the whole world a holy place. Your coming puts the muscle of faith into our daily lives. Your coming adds might to our discipleship. Your coming brings vitality to our souls. Amen.

Prayer Of Confession

We approach Christmas, O God, as people who in some way are unable. Perhaps our hope is delicate. Our choice of attitude may waver. In some, the physical body stumbles. Let us receive the strength of your blessing through the holy birth. Let us know the transformation of becoming able through newness of faith. In Jesus' name. Amen.

04B Hymns

"[O][Oh] Come, All [Ye][You] Faithful" Tune: ADESTE FIDELES
"O Word Made Flesh Among Us" Tune: BRED DINA VIDA VINGAR
"Savior Of The Nations, Come" Tune: NUN KOMM, DER HEIDEN
   HEILAND

Fourth Sunday In Advent

Gospel: Luke 1:26-38
Theme: Mary

Call To Worship
"How can this be?" Mary questioned in first response to growing the baby. Then, with the nearness of God in an angel's words, Mary came to terms with her future. When she could say, "Here I am, God," the angel knew she would be all right and departed. We come to this place filled with questions of "How can this be?" We leave mysteriously heartened that it is all right to give ourselves over to God's plans for a future and a hope.

Collect
Lead us, Holy Parent, from questions to acceptance. Move us forward beyond fear to expectation as it dawns upon us that we are an important part of your plan. Guide us in the right way our lives should go. For the sake of Jesus. Amen.

Prayer Of Confession
When you come into our lives, O great Designer, you change our future. When you walk with us, what at first seemed inconceivable and impossible by ourselves takes on a trace of hope and then a sense of certainty. Help us to listen for your plans for us and to recognize the ways you are with us as hope. Through Jesus. Amen.

04B Hymns
"[O][Oh] Come, All [Ye][You] Faithful" Tune: ADESTE FIDELES
"My Heart Sings Out With Joyful Praise" Tune: ELLACOMBE or
 MARIAS LOVSÅNG
"Born In The Night, Mary's Child" Tune: MARY'S CHILD

---

1. Sing verse three of "Now Bless The God Of Israel" after the Old Testament reading.

Christmas Eve/Day

First Lesson: Isaiah 9:2-7
Theme: Releasing Joy

Call To Worship

Leader: Let us rejoice in this day that God has made.
People: God brings joy into the world.
Leader: Let us be glad and give thanks.
People: Jesus is born.

Collect

On this day, O God, we recognize an energy that can surmount the world's problems. Let our troubles take second place to the joy that wells up within us. Let us acknowledge with lightened hearts this hope that the newborn savior brings. Amen.

Prayer Of Confession

Sometimes, O God, joy bounces and leaps. It reawakens our child-like nature. Sometimes, O God, joy is a hardy presence that permeates our whole being with quiet sustenance. However the joy of Christmas comes to us, let us welcome it with a thankful spirit. Amen.

05B Hymns

"Christians, Awake, Salute The Happy Morn" Tune: YORKSHIRE
"Unto Us A Boy Is Born" Tune: PUER NOBIS
"Joy To The World" Tune: ANTIOCH

Christmas Eve/Day

Second Lesson: Titus 2:11-14
Theme: God Who Gave

Call To Worship

Leader: It is Christmas.
People: The Holy Child has come.
Leader: God appears with the most costly gift.
People: The Holy Child has come.
Leader: God gives salvation in an infant's sigh.
All: Praise be to God. It is Christmas. Jesus has come.

Collect

We welcome you, little Holy One. We wish you well. We see how modest your beginning is, how simply your needs are met. We offer you our love in return, little Holy One. Amen.

Prayer Of Confession

Ever-giving God, may this gift of Jesus make a difference in our lives. Let us recognize your present power to save us from our negative side. Let us appreciate that we can turn away from discouragement and begin again because of your Holy Child. Amen.

05B Hymns

"Break Forth, O Beauteous Heavenly Light" Tune: ERMUNTRE DICH

"Rock-a-Bye, My Dear Little Boy" **OR** "Little Jesus, Sweetly Sleep" Tune: ROCKING

"Joy To The World" Tune: ANTIOCH

Christmas Eve/Day

Gospel: Luke 2:1-20
Theme: In These Days

Call To Worship

Leader: In those days, things were different from these days:
People: No e-mail, no interstate highways, no cars, no hospitals.
Leader: In those days, things were like these days:
People: No vacancy signs, people doing what was required of them, going about making a living, persons noticing when something significant happens.
All: In those days and in these days, the miracle of God comes into our lives.

Collect

Let us be like the shepherds of old and confirm the unexpected despite apprehension. Let our curiosity carry us onward. Let us bring a torch to see the newborn Jesus and light the way for others to come tenderly, gently this silent, holy night. Amen.

Prayer Of Confession

We come today to hear the angels sing. We gather at the stable only as curious onlookers but find the birth of Jesus has something important to do with us. Yes, both within our hymns and beyond the choir's voice, the angels sing. Amen.

05B Hymns

"Bring A Torch, Jeannette, Isabella" Tune: BRING A TORCH
"Away In A Manger" Tune: AWAY IN A MANGER
"Silent Night" Tune: STILLE NACHT

First Sunday After Christmas (Holy Family)

First Lesson: Isaiah 61:10—62:3
Theme: Called By A New Name

Call To Worship

Leader: God calls us out of our silence.
          God bids us find our voices.
          God calls us by a new name.
          This is the story of Christmas.
All: **We are God's family. Alleluia! Alleluia!**

Collect

As we gather here, O God, to sing again the tunes of Christmas, let us renew our own sense of empowerment. As members of your spiritual family, let us carry forth the songs of Christmas into the silent chasms of human misunderstanding. For the sake of Jesus. Amen.

Prayer Of Confession

In the midst of winter's constraints, embolden our hearts to leave behind what separates us from you and from each other, O God, so we might spring toward the right attitudes and the just actions of being part of your family. Amen.

06B Hymns[1]

24

First Sunday After Christmas (Holy Family)

Second Lesson: Galatians 4:4-7
Theme: Because You Are Children

Call To Worship

Wanted, chosen, adopted, family — these are the words of Christmas. By adoption, one takes a child into one's own family by legal means and raises it as one's own. Come as wanted, chosen, adopted children of God. Come with the joy of knowing we belong to God by God's choice. Come with the peace of knowing whose we are. Come with an alleluia.

Collect

You treat us not as slaves, people made into things, but as individuals of value and worth. By Jesus' example, dear God, we would live out our lives freely choosing to serve you. Amen.

Prayer Of Confession

When it comes to our children, Holy Parent, help us to differentiate between belonging to and possessing. Keep us mindful of the difference between being a servant and being a slave. Let us remember whose we are as children of God. In the name of Jesus. Amen.

06B Hymns[1]

First Sunday After Christmas (Holy Family)

Gospel: Luke 2:22-40
Theme: God's Child

Call To Worship

We think Christmas is for young families. Then we meet the very old — an Anna, a Simeon, perhaps a great-aunt who did not marry, or one to whom no children were born. Come, be like the prophetess Anna or the devout Simeon to whom, in their advanced age, God gave the gifts of hope, of seeing possibility, and of being able to recognize Christ among us.

Collect

Thank God for the eldest among us who possess the perspective to see what is important. Thank God for those who have the time to carry others in their prayers. Thank God for those who convey the persistence of hope. Through Jesus. Amen.

Prayer Of Confession

We lift up the eldest members of this church. Let those whose worn-out bodies tempt them to succumb to isolation find a way to inspire others. Let those who might yield to focusing entirely on themselves discover and share their wisdom. Let those given to surrender to the wearing down of the spirit offer encouragement to others who come their way. Amen.

06B Hymns[1]

---

1. This Sunday, try a Singing Sunday to sing congregational choices of Advent/Christmas hymns. In addition to regular hymn times, include a "Time For Singing" for singing one verse of several hymns.

Second Sunday After Christmas

First Lesson: Jeremiah 31:7-14
Theme: Firstborn

Call To Worship

Leader: With the birth of Jesus, God has become a parent. Raise shouts of praise.

People: We acknowledge you, O God, as the source of our being. We raise shouts of praise and alleluias to your holy name.

Collect

No matter if the firstborn is a birth child, an adopted child, or a loaned neighborhood child, the anticipation of a wanted child coming into the household brings joy. We look at you through different eyes now, holy Parent. We see the joy and fulfillment of your heart. You are parent, not landlord. Because of Jesus. Amen.

Prayer Of Confession

Teach us more fully, O God, what it means to be related. Teach us how to bridge distances across the dinner table, as we pass through the house, as we leave hurried notes. Teach us so we will constantly renew the message that family members are of the heart begotten. Amen.

07B Hymns

"Of The [Father's Love][Parent's Heart] Begotten" Tune: DIVINUM MYSTERIUM

"That Boy-Child Of Mary" Tune: BLANTYRE

"While Shepherds Watched Their Flocks By Night" Tune: WINCHESTER OLD

Second Sunday After Christmas

Second Lesson: Ephesians 1:3-14
Theme: Love Lavished On You

Call To Worship
God's parenting contains nothing miserly. Love is lavished on God's children, not parsimoniously dispensed to dependent underlings. A good solid start — is that not what good parenting is about? Come, receive God's love in all its abundance. Accept God's love in all your fullness.

Collect
Blessings go to you, O God, who has blessed us in Jesus with every spiritual blessing. Blessings go to you who chooses to give us Jesus. You save us with your forgiveness. You open us with your kindness. Blessings to you, O giving and merciful God. Amen.

Prayer Of Confession
We find it easier, O God, to love people in theory than to practice loving. We find it less complicated to respect others and to be kind from a distance than when we see them every day. Dear God, let the strength of your love encourage us to decide to greet those close to us with a loving spirit. For the sake of Jesus. Amen.

07B Hymns
"Love Divine, All Loves Excelling" Tune: BEECHER
"Love Came Down At Christmas" Tune: GARTAN or WHITNEY
"O Love Of God, How Strong And True" Tune: EISENACH

Second Sunday After Christmas

Gospel: John 1:1-18
Theme: God's Kids

Call To Worship

Leader: No one has ever seen God.
People: The mystery of Christmas brings us closer to God.
Leader: It is God's only Son,
People: God as clearly human as a little child.
Leader: Jesus is close to the Father's heart,
People: So close are spirit and flesh.
Leader: Jesus has made God known.
People: Jesus born at Christmas brings God to us.
All: Let us worship God with an alleluia.

Collect

As we receive Jesus, O God, you give us the power to become children of God. As we believe in the name of Jesus, you give us the power to become your children. All praise to you, Mary's child born in the night, O word made flesh among us. Through Jesus. Amen.

Prayer Of Confession

We do not know you, gracious God, when our idea of you is too small. We do not recognize you when our concept of you puts you completely beyond our reach. Hear both our wanting to be yours and our reluctance to accept the responsibility of being yours. Amen.

07B Hymns

"Born In the Night, Mary's Child" Tune: MARY'S CHILD
"O Word Made Flesh Among Us" Tune: BRED DINA VIDA VINGAR
"What Child Is This?" Tune: GREENSLEEVES

29

Epiphany Of Our Lord

First Lesson: Isaiah 60:1-6
Theme: Sonrise

Call To Worship

Leader: Day-birthing sun startles wind into unsettled gusts then, up, stands suspended. Silent, full power surveys possibility.

People: We have come for morning has broken. We have come to survey what is possible today. We are here to worship God.

Collect

We overcame the temptation to spend extra time in bed. We arose to greet your new day, O thou ever-creating God. Sunrise radiance always surprises us. This Sunday of Epiphany has begun. We give you thanks and praise your holy name. Amen.

Prayer Of Confession

Gracious God, we would do more than mark off this day on a calendar. Let us circle it and enjoy it. We would do more than yawn tentatively at the morning. Filled with expectation, let us come to the mystery of another day of life. In the name of your rising son, Jesus. Amen.

08B Hymns

"Morning Has Broken" Tune: BUNESSAN
"Faithful God, You Have Been Our Guide" Tune: LINSTEAD
"When Morning Gilds The Skies" Tune: LAUDES DOMINI

Epiphany Of Our Lord

Second Lesson: Ephesians 3:1-12
Theme: Epiphany

Call To Worship
If we knew all the answers, we would not be drawn again and
again toward the divine mystery of God's coming among us. We ar-
rive this Epiphany Sunday filled with readiness. We want to discover
anew the presence of God.

Collect
We answer mystery with hope. We regard the puzzles of your
plans for us with curiosity. We approach you, O God, with a renewed
sense of wonder at the birth and life of Jesus Christ. Amen.

Prayer Of Confession
Gracious God, give us the boldness to avoid explaining away too
much. Give us the courage to escape discarding your mysteries because of our skepticism. Amen.

08B Hymns
"Brightest And Best" Tune: MORNING STAR
"Immortal Love, Forever Full" Tune: SERENITY
"Lord, Dismiss Us With Your Blessing" Tune: REGENT SQUARE
    or SICILIAN MARINERS

Epiphany Of Our Lord

Gospel: Matthew 2:1-12
Theme: "Who Receives Your Fidelity?"

Call To Worship
The wise persons from the East brought far more than gold, myrrh, and frankincense to the Christ Child. Seeing through the schemes of King Herod, they held firm to their newly found allegiance and were loyal to the holy family. Let us consider on this Sunday of Epiphany what gifts we can bring to God.

Collect
The greatest offering we can bring to you, O God, in return for your gift of the Christ Child is to live decent, acceptable lives. We come to you today offering you the best that is within us. For the sake of Jesus. Amen.

Prayer Of Confession
Help us, O God of the faithful, to protect the faith by being people of integrity. Guide us with the illumination of your presence to recognize and overcome our negative dimensions. Aid our efforts to focus on what is right and what is good. Amen.

08B Hymns
"Go Tell It On The Mountain" Tune: GO TELL IT
"Who Would Think That What Was Needed" Tune: SCARLET
  RIBBONS
"In The Bleak Midwinter" Tune: CRANHAM

Baptism Of Our Lord

First Lesson: Genesis 1:1-5
Theme: Good For You

Call To Worship

Leader: Creation is light.
People: It is good! It is good! God sees that it is good.
Leader: Jesus' birth begins a new day.
People: God sees that it is good.
Leader: Human birth is a new beginning.
People: God sees that it is good.

Collect

May our lives continuously reflect the goodness of your creation, O God. May we discern your ever-unfolding plan for us. Take our lives, take our love, take our being. We dedicate ourselves anew to you. Amen.

Prayer Of Confession

We take for granted the light that is in our lives, O generous God, until we consider how precise is your creation of the eye and the hand. We miss how good creation is until we contemplate the resilience of the human spirit. Then, we praise you with thankful hearts. Amen.

09B Hymns

"God Of Earth And Sea And Heaven" Tune: LLANSANNAN
"Take My Life, [God][And Let It Be]" Tune: VIENNA
"God Created Heaven And Earth" Tune: TOA-SIA

Baptism Of Our Lord

Second Lesson: Acts 19:1-7
Theme: Getting It Straight

Call To Worship

Leader: This is the place for beginning the lifelong journey of clarifying our faith.

People: We come here to worship God and to reach toward spiritual growth.

Leader: Like the need of early Christians to grasp the meaning of baptism, we come with many faith questions and misconceptions.

People: We come here to get things straight.

Collect

What is it, God, this Holy Spirit? What are the lasting truths about our Christian faith? Many varieties of belief flood our wondering. Accept our questions as expressions of wanting to know you and your newly baptized Son. Amen.

Prayer Of Confession

Not all of us have heard in the heart the words of our faith, O God. Help us to listen with the soul as well as with the mind. We need to get it straight so we can discard useless beliefs and begin to cherish the treasures of a maturing Christian faith. Let us be undaunted by matters of the Spirit that cannot be confirmed by our senses. Amen.

09B Hymns

"Breathe On Me, Breath Of God" Tune: TRENTHAM

"Into My Heart, Lord Jesus" Tune: Response

"Come, Holy Spirit, God And Lord! Tune: DAS NEUGEBORNE KINDELEIN

Baptism Of Our Lord

Gospel: Mark 1:4-11
Theme: Just A Few Drops Of Water

Call To Worship

Leader: Quiet baptismal water connects us to God forever.
People: Just a few drops of water.
Leader: In a moment of meeting, the mystery replays.
People: Just a few drops of water.
Leader: Together, we lift up God's creation.
People: Baptism — just a few drops of water.

Collect

The frowns soften from our faces, dear God, as we remember the promises we have made and the baptismal commitments others made on our behalf. The smiles rise as we hear again the bridging words of blessing that bring forgiveness and freedom. Amen.

Prayer Of Confession

God, return us to a sense of the holy. Restore to us the awareness of our holiness. Renew us with the remembering of just a few drops of baptismal water. In the name of the Creator, the Savior, and the Sustainer. Amen.

09B Hymns

"Jesus Calls Us, O'er The Tumult" Tune: ST. ANDREW
"Send Down Thy Truth, O God" Tune: ST. MICHAEL
"Lord, Make Me More Holy" Tune: LORD, MAKE ME MORE HOLY

Second Sunday After Epiphany

First Lesson: 1 Samuel 3:1-10 (11-20)
Theme: Both Ears Tingling

Call To Worship

Leader: We listen for the way God calls to us.

People: Would that God spoke so clearly that both of our ears were set to tingling.

Leader: In the child Samuel, God chose someone who did not yet know God enough to recognize God.

People: Samuel was lucky. Samuel was ready to listen when God called him by name.

Collect

We come to you, O God, half wondering what message you would give us were you to gain our attention. Teach us to listen. Help us be as persistent children in perceiving your call. Teach us to be as straightforward as Samuel in answering, "Here I am." Amen.

Prayer Of Confession

We are grateful, O God, that you keep track of us. We are thankful that you call us by name. You have enough concern about the individuals of your creation to give each one your attention. You call repeatedly until we realize it is you summoning us. Amen.

10B Hymns

"Before Jehovah's Aweful Throne" Tune: OLD HUNDREDTH or WINCHESTER NEW
"Like A Mother Who Has Borne Us" Tune: AUSTIN
"Here I Am, Lord" Tune: HERE I AM, LORD

Second Sunday After Epiphany

Second Lesson: 1 Corinthians 6:12-20
Theme: Not Our Own

Call To Worship
Come into the holiness of this place that has been dedicated to the worship of God. Come here as people recognizing the holy unity of body, mind, and spirit. Come as people united in spirit with God.

Collect
We welcome the unity we share with you in spirit, O God. May the respect and care we offer you reveal itself in the way we treat our bodies. Let the actions of our whole being reflect our praise of you. In the name of Jesus. Amen.

Prayer Of Confession
Forgive us, O merciful God, when we ignore that anything harmful we do to our body also damages our innermost being. You are so close to us that when we hurt ourselves we also hurt you. Forgive us when we forget that. Increase our understanding that anyone united to God becomes one in spirit with God. Through the Holy Spirit. Amen.

10B Hymns
"O God, Thou Art The Father" Tune: DURROW
"I Am [Thine][Yours], O Lord" Tune: I AM [THINE][YOURS]
"Forth In [Thy][Your] Name, O Lord, I Go" Tune: LAKEWOOD or
  MORNING HYMN

Second Sunday After Epiphany

Gospel: John 1:43-51
Theme: Nathanael

Call To Worship

Leader: Cynicism, wariness, distrust, doubt — the attitudes of Nathanael's time also are words of our time.

People: Surrounded by the safety of people who have chosen faith, we come here to make known our questions.

Leader: Are our words of uncertainty a protective impulse or a yielding of attitude choice?

People: We come here to find encouragement as we increase our faith.

Collect

We choose, O God, to shed the negative attitudes that thwart our journey into faith. For the sake of Jesus. Amen.

Prayer Of Confession

We think we go about our lives largely unobserved, O God. Then we discover how much we reveal through body language, facial expressions, the gait of our walk, the activities we choose, and the places we go. Lead us toward being equally transparent in the living out of our faith. In the name of Jesus. Amen.

10B Hymns

"As With Gladness [Men][Those] Of Old" Tune: DIX

"[All][He] Who Would Valiant Be" Tune: MONKS GATE or ST. DUNSTAN

"Once In Royal David's City" Tune: IRBY

Third Sunday After Epiphany

First Lesson: Jonah 3:1-5, 10
Theme: Get Up

Call To Worship
Know that God pays attention to our attempts to improve our lives, our community, and our world. Know that our Creator gives us credit for the modest steps we take as well as for the complete changing of our ways. Therefore, let us be encouraged as we come to worship God.

Collect
Your compassion leads us forward, O merciful Sustainer. With your acceptance of our smallest efforts, we feel encouraged to strengthen the good within ourselves and rekindle our hope for the world community. Through your Spirit. Amen.

Prayer Of Confession
You know our reservations, O God. We concoct long lists of conditions when we really do not want to change. We ask for your help in overcoming our reticence to act before a problem presents itself as an ultimatum. Amen.

11B Hymns
"God The Omnipotent" Tune: RUSSIAN HYMN
"Give To The Winds Thy Fears" Tune: ST. BRIDE
"O Day Of God, Draw [Near][Nigh]" Tune: ST. MICHAEL

Third Sunday After Epiphany

Second Lesson: 1 Corinthians 7:29-31
Theme: Impending Change

Call To Worship
Come, let us worship the one eternal God whose presence and constancy we can count on despite any change that comes our way.

Collect
To meet change, O God, we choose faith rather than confusion. We trust the precepts of our faith as we navigate the chaos and the epiphanies of the unknown. We continue on because you are with us. Through the Holy Spirit. Amen.

Prayer Of Confession
When impending change looms, help us be faithful to our promises, O eternal God. Remind us of the endurance of our faith that outlasts the commotion that comes with change. Guide our actions so we will stay level-headed and steady-hearted. Amen.

11B Hymns
"Be [Now][Thou] My Vision" or "Christ Be My Leader" Tune: SLANE
"Christian, Rise And Act [Thy][Your] Creed" Tune: INNOCENTS
"Faith Of [Our Fathers][The Martyrs]" Tune: ST. CATHERINE

Third Sunday After Epiphany

Gospel: Mark 1:14-20
Theme: Fishing

Call To Worship

Leader: Fishing — fishing for a catch of followers.
People: Fishing for positive attitudes.
Leader: For the truths of our faith.
People: For a second chance.
Leader: For talent.
People: Fishing for wisdom.
Leader: Fishing for hope.
People: Fishing for God.
All: Let's come fishing.

Collect

We would go fishing for the faith, O God, by telling the good news rather than fish stories. We would go fishing with the right story instead of empty promises. We would let our lives endorse the creed we follow. In the name of Jesus the Christ. Amen.

Prayer Of Confession

Teach us how to say "Yes" when you come fishing for us, God. For the sake of Jesus. Amen.

11B Hymns

"Christ For The World We Sing!" Tune: ITALIAN HYMN
"I Love To Tell The Story" Tune: HANKEY
"Rise Up, O [Men][Church] Of God" Tune: FESTAL SONG

Fourth Sunday After Epiphany

First Lesson: Deuteronomy 18:15-20
Theme: Words In Your Mouth

Call To Worship
Come and worship. Worship the God of truth who is present in our innermost hearts and who offers guidance in every aspect of our lives.

Collect
We come to you, O God, aware of your trust in us as speakers for you. Let the truths we illustrate through our actions be worthy of this trust. Let the attitudes we portray through our relationships with others be honorable. Let the words that come from our mouths reflect oneness with you. Amen.

Prayer Of Confession
We come to this place, O Sustainer, where we can admit to feeling vulnerability as human beings. We wish that you would put words into our mouths. We struggle with knowing the right thing to say. We ask this day to trust the soundness of our integrity and to remember that you, O God, are a mighty fortress and our strong salvation. Amen.

12B Hymns
"God Is My Strong Salvation" Tune: MEIN LEBEN
"Many Are The Lightbeams" Tune: LIGHTBEAMS
"A Mighty Fortress Is Our God" Tune: EIN' FESTE BURG

Fourth Sunday After Epiphany

Second Lesson: 1 Corinthians 8:1-13
Theme: Puff Or Love?

Call To Worship
Are you full of puff or love? "Knowledge puffs up, but love builds up," says the apostle Paul. Certainly, we qualify, Paul must mean knowledge without wisdom. Surely, he suggests that knowledge is troublesome without love.

Collect
We come to you, O God, reminded that we must put love before all else in the command to love our neighbor as ourselves. For the sake of Jesus. Amen.

Prayer Of Confession
God who created the human mind, let us acquire knowledge for the right reasons. Keep us from puffing up with self-importance. Keep us from strutting with long words and separating language that interferes with neighborly conversations. Help us avoid using our knowledge in ways that cause others to feel unfit. In our journey as Christians, let love season all that we do. In the name of Christ. Amen.

12B Hymns
"Love Came Down At Christmas" Tune: GARTAN or WHITNEY
"Lord, I Want To Be A Christian" Tune: I WANT TO BE A
    CHRISTIAN
"For The Healing Of The Nations" Tune: CWM RHONDDA

43

Fourth Sunday After Epiphany

Gospel: Mark 1:21-28
Theme: Influence

Call To Worship
Internet authority alerts us to the differences between empty power and valid presence. Jesus' authority invites our mindfulness of his source and his oneness of purpose. Come, let us worship the one, true God.

Collect
These days, O God, when the term "authority figure" signals more dismissal than dignity, we reaffirm our faith in Jesus as the one to follow. Amen.

Prayer Of Confession
We appreciate the power those whom we influence give us, O God. Guide us lest we snatch authority without knowing what we are doing. Teach us to ask the right questions before we give sanctuary to anyone who assumes authority. Ground our power in the principles of the Christian faith. Amen.

12B Hymns
"How Firm A Foundation" Tune: ADESTE FIDELES
"Silence! Frenzied, Unclean Spirit" Tune: AUTHORITY
"Tell Out, My Soul" Tune: WOODLANDS

Fifth Sunday After Epiphany

First Lesson: Isaiah 40:21-31
Theme: Waiting For God

Call To Worship
"Even youths will faint and be weary, and the young will fall exhausted; but those who wait for God shall renew their strength, they shall mount up with wings like eagles, they shall run and not be weary, they shall walk and not faint." Wait, I say, for the Savior.

Collect
Here in this hour, O sustaining Creator, we delay our haste to keep pace with the volume of demands shouting at us. Here we pause for spiritual rest. Here we wait for you. Here we begin to anticipate renewal of our strength. Thank you, God. Amen.

Prayer Of Confession
Teach us the right way to await you, O God. Sustain us as we practice enduring and resolute patience. Let us pause well so that in our tarrying our very souls begin to lap up vigor. When we feel powerless, teach us to expect you who has the capacity to understand, to lift up, and to empower. Amen.

13B Hymns
"Be [Calm][Still], My Soul" Tune: FINLANDIA
"Wellspring Of Wisdom" Tune: WELLSPRING
"Leaning On The Everlasting Arms" Tune: LEANING or SHOW
    ALTER

Fifth Sunday After Epiphany

Second Lesson: 1 Corinthians 9:16-23
Theme: When In Rome

Call To Worship
Christians come here to worship God who has entrusted us with being advocates for the faith. Let us be worthy champions of God.

Collect
As Christians, we hold a delicate power. We would be catalysts for Christian nurture. We would be inclusive rather than exclusive. We would be welcomers. For the sake of Christ. Amen.

Prayer Of Confession
Guide us, O God, to ascertain what we are doing so we will remain faithful to the healing of others. Let us escape becoming coercive or haughty in our winning over of others. Grant us sensitivity as we find the best ways to reach out without losing our integrity or our identity. In the name of Jesus. Amen.

13B Hymns
"[O][Oh] For A Thousand Tongues To Sing" Tune: AZMON or
    BEATITUDO
"Make Me A Captive, Lord" Tune: DIADEMATA
"A Charge To Keep I Have" Tune: BOYLSTON

Fifth Sunday After Epiphany

Gospel: Mark 1:29-39
Theme: Bone Weary

Call To Worship
We celebrate the remembering of our homes as places of healing. We lift up the hope of increasing in our families a climate that elevates restoration and rejuvenation so we might go about our work with renewed vigor.

Collect
We would be a connecting people who carry hope and a sense of community with us wherever we are. We are grateful for the places we call home — a borrowed spot of a friend, an apartment, a house with a garden, somewhere we feel welcome, a place to receive and a place to give. In Jesus' name. Amen.

Prayer Of Confession
When we are bone weary, God, we need a room to come to. Our temptation is to make our dwelling places into isolating cocoons where we passively hide out. Help us, rather, to find ways to give our homes an environment that nourishes, fortifies, and prepares us for reconnecting with the world. In the spirit of Jesus. Amen.

13B Hymns
"Amazing Grace, How Sweet The Sound" Tune: AMAZING GRACE
"God, Bless Our Homes" Tune: CHARTERHOUSE
"Immortal Love, Forever Full" Tune: SERENITY

Sixth Sunday After Epiphany

First Lesson: 2 Kings 5:1-14
Theme: If Only ...

Call To Worship
Are you an "If only" person or a "Well, maybe" person? Are you a wistful thinker whose voice pinches with regret? Or does the hope of possibility stir within you despite obstacles? Hear the call to worship a God of possibility. Come, let us worship God.

Collect
When we are near you, gracious Sustainer, we reach beyond the average. When your Spirit heartens us, our own expectations awaken and stretch. We give praise to you, O God, for the vigor you provide. Amen.

Prayer Of Confession
Slip the whisper of hope into our hearts, O God, when we wonder how we possibly can do what appears ahead of us. Turn us from discouraging thoughts and focus on obstacles. Lead us toward spending creative energy on finding the way to do what we thought we never could. Amen.

14B Hymns
"Awake, My Soul, Stretch Every Nerve" Tune: CHRISTMAS
"God's Glory Is A Wondrous Thing" Tune: HUMMEL
"God Hath Spoken By The Prophets" or "Thy Strong Word" Tune: EBENEZER

Sixth Sunday After Epiphany

Second Lesson: 1 Corinthians 9:24-27
Theme: Give Of Your Best

Call To Worship
Let us enter the house of God with a mind to make decisions that will keep our faith vital in an ever-changing world. Come, let us worship God.

Collect
We reaffirm here, O God, our intention to live with the goal of prevailing. We plan to do better at anchoring the important work of being Christian. Our aim is to increase self-discipline so we might reach toward the promises we hold. Amen.

Prayer Of Confession
Move us forward, O God, beyond giving up, lest we fail before we try. Move us away from wasting energy in aimless abandon before we come to cherish only a remnant of vitality. Inspire us to do our best without worrying about being inadequate, O God. For the sake of Christ. Amen.

14B Hymns
"Spirit, Spirit Of Gentleness" Tune: SPIRIT
"Give Of Your Best To The Master" Tune: Unknown **OR** "Fight The Good Fight" Tune: GRACE CHURCH, GANANOQUE or PENTECOST
"I Sing A Song Of The Saints Of God" Tune: GRAND ISLE

Sixth Sunday After Epiphany

Gospel: Mark 1:40-45
Theme: "I Do Choose"

Call To Worship

Leader: If you choose, O God,
People: To hear the prayers we offer,
To be a catalyst for healing powers within us,
To be present for us —
Leader: I do choose, O my People,
People: To care immediately for your needs when you come to me,
To see that you are as healthy as you can be,
To be at your side.
Leader: I do choose to believe that you are worthy.

Collect

To You who chooses to help us clean up our lives, we come by choice. We could have gone elsewhere to charlatan or fraud, but we trust your choosing to lead us. In the name of Jesus. Amen.

Prayer Of Confession

Grant to us the inclination to come to you, O God, with our troubles. Increase our faith in your capacity to view each human being as your valuable creation. Amen.

14B Hymns

"He Leadeth Me, O Blessed Thought" Tune: HE LEADETH ME
"Father, Hear The Prayer We Offer" Tune: REGENSBURG
"O Young And Fearless Prophet" Tune: BLAIRGOWRIE

Seventh Sunday After Epiphany

First Lesson: Isaiah 43:18-25
Theme: The Blotter

Call To Worship
Know that God sees more than our falling short when God looks at us. Know that God is a God of possibility who sees new things in us. Rejoice, therefore, in the grace and hope God offers as nourishment for our souls.

Collect
O God who makes a way in our wildernesses, hear our prayers of praise. To you, who has chosen us as your own, we rededicate our lives. In you, we find reason to hope. Amen.

Prayer Of Confession
If you do not remember our sins, O gracious One, then once we have admitted them and asked your forgiveness, grace us also to forget them. Assist us as we seek to leave behind what is over. Guide us as we strive to make headway in the way we live. Through the name of Jesus. Amen.

15B Hymns
"Praise To God, Immortal Praise" Tune: DIX
"Let Us Hope When Hope Seems Hopeless" Tune: LET US HOPE
"God's Eye Is On The Sparrow" Tune: SPARROW

Seventh Sunday After Epiphany

Second Lesson: 2 Corinthians 1:18-22
Theme: Yes!

Call To Worship

Leader: Every one of God's promises is a "Yes." God says "Yes" to
          your being. Consider today what it means for you that God
          has put God's own seal on you.

People: Let us praise our creator and sustainer.

Collect

All around us, O Provider, is evidence of your acceptance and
hope for our future. We, your chosen people, gather with grateful
hearts. Hear our singing to you the spirited songs of affirmation. In
the name of Christ. Amen.

Prayer Of Confession

Surely, O God whose faithfulness to us is so great that you provide a daily cornucopia of hope, strength, and compassion, surely we
can sing "Yes" to our own being. Through your gracious Spirit. Amen.

15B Hymns

"Great Is Your Faithfulness" Tune: FAITHFULNESS

"Your Chosen People" Tune: AURELIA

"I'm Pressing On The Upward Way" or "Higher Ground" Tune:
HIGHER GROUND

Seventh Sunday After Epiphany

Gospel: Mark 2:1-12
Theme: It's About Forgiveness

Call To Worship

Leader: Sin imprisons us within ourselves. A huge barrier stands between us and others.

People: Forgiveness brings freedom.

Leader: Sin keeps us from relating to our neighbor. It closes us from giving love and from receiving respect.

People: Forgiveness brings openness.

Leader: Sin immobilizes our spirit. We give up on ourselves and no longer try.

People: Forgiveness brings hope.

All: Praise be to the Creator who forgives.

Collect

You send us to help others, O merciful God, when they are helpless. As your people, we would strive to become aware of those whose spirits have become frozen. We would bring them to those who can make a difference in their lives. Amen.

Prayer Of Confession

We sin, O God, if we do not also forgive. When people have wronged us or hurt those we love, we must forgive them. Only then can we return to hope, become open again toward others, and know freedom. Help us to overcome sin with forgiveness. Amen.

15B Hymns

"Praise The Lord, His Glories Show" Tune: LLANFAIR
"O Master Workman Of The Race" Tune: KINGSFOLD
"If [Thou][You] But Suffer God To Guide [Thee][You]" Tune: NEUMARK

Eighth Sunday After Epiphany

First Lesson: Hosea 2:14-20
Theme: A Door Of Hope

Call To Worship

Leader: God comes into the dry wilderness valleys of our lives and shows us a doorway to hope.

People: God has the power to transform drunken driver streets into areas of just and right action.

Leader: God shows constancy in love and faithfulness that gives us courage to commit to the hope of lasting relationships.

All: Our praise goes to you, most merciful Sustainer.

Collect

Eternal God, because of your devoted and compassionate ways, we can expect to find renewal of hope and to be restored as transmitters of hope. In the Spirit of God. Amen.

Prayer Of Confession

Life happenings bring us into valleys where water and vegetation are absent. Steep mountainous walls close off the nurture of sunshine. Speak tenderly to our souls, O Holy One, so our awareness may awaken to see the doors of hope that you faithfully provide within these valleys. Amen.

16B Hymns

"O For A World" Tune: AZMON
"How Lovely Is Your Dwelling" Tune: ES IST EIN' ROS'
"Now Is The Time Approaching" Tune: WEBB

Eighth Sunday After Epiphany

Second Lesson: 2 Corinthians 3:1-6
Theme: Letter Of Recommendation

Call To Worship

Leader: How closely intertwined is confidence with competence.
People: Be our strength, O God.
Leader: Be assured that in God's sight you need no letter of recommendation.
People: Be our strength, O God.
Leader: Take a new hold on the abilities that are yours.
People: Be our strength, O God.
Leader: Prize your gifts as signs of hope from a hopeful God.
People: Let us sing praise to God.

Collect

Let the way we live out our lives be its own letter of recommendation. Let our awareness of God's movement in our lives bolster both our courage and our oneness of purpose. Let us live beyond the letter of the law to honor the renewed promises of the heart for which you are the source, O God. Amen.

Prayer Of Confession

Enmeshed in a world that seems to expect far more of us than we can give, we sometimes feel inept, O God. Help us keep in mind the approval you give us through the vitality of your always present Spirit. In Christ. Amen.

16B Hymns

"God Moves In A Mysterious Way" Tune: DUNDEE
"God Of Our Life, Through All The Circling Years" Tune: SANDON
"Now Thank We All Our God" Tune: NUN DANKET

Eighth Sunday After Epiphany

Gospel: Mark 2:13-22
Theme: New Is New

Call To Worship

New is new. It still wears the price tag. It still feels unworn. Without blemish, it shines. The much-used cannot take the strain the new imposes upon it. The threads let go. The sinew gives way. The spirit breaks.

Collect

We make ready for the new, O ever-providing God, by sewing a new wineskin. For the sake of Christ. Amen.

Prayer Of Confession

Is it always true, O God, that we must throw out the old before we can follow what is new? We do not want to be wasteful. We do not want to become useless and replaced. We resist the changes of the unknown new. Guide us so we can greet the new with enthusiasm rather than meet it with defeat. Amen.

16B Hymns

"Immortal, Invisible, God Only Wise" Tune: ST. DENIO
"Are Ye Able" Tune: BEACON HILL
"Rescue The Perishing" Tune: RESCUE

Transfiguration Of Our Lord

First Lesson: 2 Kings 2:1-12
Theme: I Will Not Leave You

Call To Worship

Leader: Join me in this conversation about change: You must stay
here.
People: **I will not leave you.**
Leader: I must go.
People: **Be silent. I don't want to talk about it.**
Leader: Change happens.
People: **Yes, I know. Let's not discuss it.**
Leader: Change is difficult.
People: **It is hard to let go.**

Collect

In the letting go days when our souls are bruised, you send the
support of those who care about us, O Sustainer. In scary times of
unwilling transition as well as other designed life passages, you ac-
company us. We move ahead within the guidance of your gracious
Spirit. Amen.

Prayer Of Confession

During the hard times of letting go, dear God, let us surround the
suffering with understanding. Let us embrace them with what is real
and give them hugs of assurance. Let us speak honestly, then give
others space to meet the change in their own way. Within the strength
of your Spirit. Amen.

18B Hymns

"God Of The Prophets" Tune: OLD 124TH or TOULON
"Father, Hear The Prayer We Offer" Tune: REGENSBURG
"God Made From One Blood" Tune: ST. DENIO

Transfiguration Of Our Lord

Second Lesson: 2 Corinthians 4:3-6
Theme: god or God?

Call To Worship
Come and worship the God who said, "Let light shine out of darkness." Leave behind the veiling god of this world who attempts to keep you from seeing the light of Jesus Christ. Know that through the transfiguration of Jesus we are also changed forever.

Collect
We are here, O God, because your light has shone in our hearts. We have come with opened eyes, surprised but ready to receive your changing light. Through the transfiguration of Jesus. Amen.

Prayer Of Confession
Help us to keep straight, O God, which light is glitter and which light transfigures. Remind us that transfiguration is not we announcing the glory of ourselves but the disclosure of Jesus as our savior. Amen.

18B Hymns
"Lead Us, O Father" Tune: LANGRAN
"This Little Light Of Mine" Tune: LATTIMER
"Let There Be Light, O God of Hosts!" Tune: PENTECOST

Transfiguration Of Our Lord

Gospel: Mark 9:2-9
Theme: What Makes You Change?

Call To Worship

Leader: What changes us?
People: What *demands* that we change?
Leader: What *causes* change?
People: What *lets* us change?
Leader: Our responses are as varied as the people gathered here. We can say this for certain about profound change: When it comes to us, we hardly recognize ourselves yet, mysteriously, in our depths remain the same.

Collect

In an endless epiphany, change presents its surprises. Grateful for your nearness, O God, we feel better equipped to meet change. Walk us through the changes we choose and through those that we do not expect. Amen.

Prayer Of Confession

Give us courage, O eternal Spirit, to welcome the stranger we become to ourselves because of significant changes. Give us a view of change as enlarging who we are. Move us toward self-approval because of your acceptance of us. Through Jesus. Amen.

18B Hymns

"[Ye][You] Servants Of God, Your [Master][Sovereign] Proclaim" Tune: HANOVER

"O [Master][Savior], Let Me Walk With [Thee][You]" Tune: MARYTON

"Where Cross The Crowded Ways Of Life" Tune: GERMANY

Ash Wednesday

First Lesson: Joel 2:1-2, 12-17
Theme: Sound The Alarm

Call To Worship
It is Ash Wednesday. The black ashes remind us of life changed forever. The alarm sounding on the mountain is too loud, too clear, for anyone to ignore. This change will make a difference. Hear in your heart this call from God. Return to God.

Collect
We dare to return to you, O God, knowing that you are gracious and merciful. You are kind. Your love overflows. You relent from punishing. So we turn to you as honestly as we are able. For the sake of Jesus and for our sake. Amen.

Prayer Of Confession
We cannot waste energy by returning to you halfheartedly, God. We must return with all our heart when we hear you calling. Help us to realize that we, too, are part of Lent. Lent is more than a commemoration. The ageless stories and truths of Lent are also about us — from infant to child to adult to the aged. Amen.

19B Hymns
"Return, My People" Tune: REPTON
"Deep In The Shadows Of The Past" or "The Lord Is Rich And Merciful" Tune: SHEPHERDS' PIPES
"Thou Didst Leave Thy Throne" Tune: MARGARET

Ash Wednesday

Second Lesson: 2 Corinthians 5:20b—6:10
Theme: God's Servants

Call To Worship

To worship faithfully is to love each other. As this season of Lent begins, let us look around our homes, our schools, our places of work, and our community for those who need a friend. Let us be the church to others. Let us extend the grace of God to others because we ourselves are constant recipients of God's grace.

Collect

Grant us both courage and patience, O God, to stand at another's door and knock. Grant us enough caring to notice when we might be of help. Grant us the strength to be as Christ for others. Amen.

Prayer Of Confession

You, O gracious One, see our smallest attempts to be your servants in the service of others. Remind us that we represent Christ each time we extend kindness, whenever we show patience, and whenever we dare to stand up for what is right. In the name of Jesus. Amen.

19B Hymns

"O Jesus, Thou Art Standing" Tune: ST. HILDA
"What A Friend We Have In Jesus" Tune: CONVERSE or ERIE
"Children Of God" or "O Brother Man, Fold To Thy Heart" Tune: INTERCESSOR or WELWYN

Ash Wednesday

Gospel: Matthew 6:1-6, 16-21
Theme: Begin To Pray

Call To Worship
Ash Wednesday is the time to review our regrets. Ash Wednesday is the time to reach out quietly with loving kindness beyond ourselves to others. Ash Wednesday is the time to begin again to pray.

Collect
Teach us to pray for the right reasons, O God. Give us the boldness to talk to you about what is on our minds. We would turn to Jesus during this Lenten season hoping for the renewal of our lives and our focus of mission as Christian folk. Amen.

Prayer Of Confession
Leader: We have good intentions, God. Surely, if Jesus could do all he has done for us, we can find a little time to pray.

People: **We do plan to pray, God. We start out to pray regularly, then soon forget about it. Then the Lenten season moves on with only our twinges of guilt.**

Leader: Forgive us, God, for being so busy, so lazy, so thinking that our prayers always must take the shape of words.

All: **Teach us about the silent, waiting moment that gives you the opening to be mysteriously present in our lives. In Jesus' name. Amen.**

19B Hymns
"Behold Us, Lord, A Little Space" Tune: DUNFERMLINE or WINCHESTER OLD
"Father, In Thy Mysterious Presence" Tune: DONNE SECOURS
"Lord, Who Throughout These Forty Days" Tune: LAND OF REST

First Sunday In Lent

First Lesson: Genesis 9:8-17
Theme: Never Again

Call To Worship

Leader: When all seems hopeless, there God is.
People: When broken relationships smash human dreams,
Leader: When all seems hopeless, God intervenes for now and for all future generations.
People: When no one dares come forward to bridge chasms of misunderstanding,
Leader: When all seems hopeless, God offers the rainbow.

Collect

Loving God, your constancy encourages us to move toward listening, understanding, and connecting with those with whom we appear to share no point of empathy. We need the acceptance of your rainbow signs. We need the goodwill of your promises. Amen.

Prayer Of Confession

Never again, we promise. Then we utter ill-treating words in a mean moment. Never again, we vow. Then we get tired or let jealousy rise, and we speak with hurtful tones. We do not do a good job of keeping our promises, God. Help us to be more like you. Help us to honor our promises of "never again." Amen.

20B Hymns[1]

"In The Midst Of New Dimensions" Tune: NEW DIMENSIONS
"Just As I Am" Tune: WOODWORTH
"Let Us Hope When Hope Seems Hopeless" Tune: LET US HOPE[2]

First Sunday In Lent

Second Lesson: 1 Peter 3:18-22
Theme: Saved

Call To Worship
Come to worship reminded during these days and nights of Lent that through all of our struggles God acts on our behalf and for our welfare.

Collect
We pray to you, O saving God, aware that the suffering of Christ was to bring us closer to you. As you raised Christ out of the depths, so do you enter our turmoil and lift us from despair. In the name of Christ. Amen.

Prayer Of Confession
We yearn to return to you, O God. We reach out in the dark hoping by chance to find you. Then we discover you have been waiting for us all along. You wait to return us to the saving, life-giving spirit of our baptism. Through the suffering of Christ. Amen.

20B Hymns[1]
"[Born][Son] Of God, Eternal Savior" Tune: IN BABILONE or
   WEISSE FLAGGEN
"Out Of The Depths I Cry To You" Tune: AUS TIEFER NOT
"Lord, Save Thy World" or "Creator Of The Earth And Skies" Tune:
   UFFINGHAM

First Sunday In Lent

Gospel: Mark 1:9-15
Theme: Forty

Call To Worship

Leader: Forty days and forty nights, the rains came tumbling down during the great flood. Forty days and forty nights, Jesus endured the wilderness. Forty.

People: Forty. A long time to wait. A long time to be patient. A long time to learn.

Leader: Forty days of Lent. Time enough to reflect and become re-acquainted with ourselves. Time enough to gather wisdom. Time enough to know we are God's beloved. Come, let us begin.

Collect

O God, for whom rainbows and doves, floods and baptism, being afloat and bewildered, and a nimble Spirit coming are all related, it is you who sends hope when hope seems hopeless. Thank you. Amen.

Prayer Of Confession

But, God, forty days in Bible times represented a generation — a day for a year of wandering, a year of life. Will temptation never end? Will the resolution of friction ever subside? Will we ever fully know ourselves or you? Grant us hope when hope seems hopeless. Amen.

20B Hymns[1]

"Forty Days And Forty Nights" Tune: HEINLEIN
"O God, How We Have Wandered" Tune: PASSION CHORALE
"Lord Jesus, Who Through Forty Days" Tune: ST. FLAVIAN

---

1. As an introduction to the time of prayer, throughout the Sundays of Lent sing "When Jesus Wept" Tune: WHEN JESUS WEPT as a congregational canon.

2. Sing "Let Us Hope When Hope Seems Hopeless" Tune: LET US HOPE as a Lenten theme hymn the first Sunday. Then throughout Lent select one verse as a closing response before the benediction.

Second Sunday In Lent

First Lesson: Genesis 17:1-7, 15-16
Theme: Name Change

Call To Worship
So great was the change to come in the lives of Abram and Sarai that they became as new people. God gave them different names. To the casual ear, "Abraham" is not so unlike "Abram" and "Sarai" is similar to "Sarah," yet they knew their lives were changed forever. As we worship today, let us reflect upon the signs of God's activity in our lives.

Collect
We would be listening, O God, for your voice. Help us quiet unimportant ambitions that reach out no further than ourselves so that we might allow the ideas of your eternal Spirit to speak. We want to be as true as we can to your hopes for us. In the name of Christ. Amen.

Prayer Of Confession
Like pondering the choice of a unique e-mail identity, we consider the best expression of our being, O God. Our names hold a lifetime of stories, yet you continue to surprise us with plans that bring us renewal. Grant us a keenness of spirit so that we might be aware of the significance of the smallest change of a name. Amen.

21B Hymns
"The God Of Abraham Praise" Tune: LEONI or YIGDAL
"I Would Be True" Tune: PEEK
"Let Us Hope When Hope Seems Hopeless" Tune: LET US HOPE

Second Sunday In Lent

Second Lesson: Romans 4:13-25
Theme: Promises, Promises

Call To Worship

Promises, promises — empty words? Promises, the fullest of words. It will happen, says the promise God makes. Come, believe the promises of a faithful God.

Collect

God, you grace-filled artist, you find the smallest piece of life within us and raise it up. You grow hope into reality where we see only mirage. You call into existence the things that do not exist. O Thou, who keeps your promises. Amen.

Prayer Of Confession

Stretch our faith, O God, so we will expect to keep the promises we make. Expand our trust in you, so we will come through the unfruitful, Lenten times in our lives to give birth to an alleluia. Amen.

21B Hymns

"Guide Me, O [My Great Redeemer][Thou Great Jehovah]" Tune: CWM RHONDDA or ZION

"O Jesus, I Have Promised" or "O Savior, Precious Savior" Tune: ANGEL'S STORY

"God Of Abraham And Sarah" Tune: CONSTANTINE

Second Sunday In Lent

Gospel: Mark 8:31-38
Theme: Get Out Of The Way

Call To Worship

Leader: We must tell Satan to get out of the way so we can move forward.

People: Get behind me, Satan!

Leader: We must stand up to negative, destructive temptation. We must aim our energy toward that which heals and is constructive.

People: Get behind me, Satan!

Collect

We stand before your cross, O sacrificing God, aware that conflicting choices press upon us. As we begin to appreciate the brave choices Jesus made, let us renew the decision to be his followers. Amen.

Prayer Of Confession

The changes you ask of us, O God, seem impossible. Like Peter, we do not even want to hear uncomfortable words. Forgive us when we are selfish. We consider denying ourselves but find too many things we do not want to give up. Forgive us for putting so much importance on human things. Help us to make room in our lives for the way of Christ. Amen.

21B Hymns

"Before Your Cross, O Jesus" Tune: ST. CHRISTOPHER
"Strengthen All The Weary Hands" Tune: SONG OF REJOICING
" 'Take Up Your Cross,' The Savior Said" Tune: DEUS TUORUM MILITUM or NUN LAST UNS DEN LEIB BEGRABEN or "Take Up Thy Cross" Tune: GERMANY

Third Sunday In Lent

First Lesson: Exodus 20:1-17
Theme: You Shall ...

Call To Worship

Leader: God said, You shall worship only me and worship me in the right way. Without idols, false gods, or forgetting the sabbath.

People: **God said, You shall live in right relationship with your family, your neighbor, and the rest of the world. Without murder, adultery, stealing, bearing false witness, or coveting of anything that belongs to someone else.**

Collect

Turn us toward realizing what it means to honor you, All-powerful God, and our neighbors in right relationship. Heal our world through a renewed sense of respect — one person for another, one nation for another, one faith for another. Help us become responsible for our attitudes and actions. Amen.

Prayer Of Confession

We live in days of disrespect and find sport in dishonoring. Give us courage to move from deadening fear to life-giving hope. One by one, let us initiate attitudes of respect and honor. Amen.

22B Hymns

"God The Omnipotent!" Tune: RUSSIAN HYMN
"For The Healing Of The Nations" Tune: WESTMINSTER ABBEY
"Lead On [Eternal Sovereign], [O King Eternal] Tune: LANCASHIRE

Third Sunday In Lent

Second Lesson: 1 Corinthians 1:18-25
Theme: God's Foolishness

Call To Worship

Leader: When God became knowable to us as a vulnerable baby, our wisdom may have concluded, how powerless. The world had not considered the disarming power of love.

People: **As the crucifixion evolved and God did not stop Jesus' death, our strength may have judged, this is no way to change things. The world had not weighed the transformation love can engender.**

All: **We honor the power and wisdom of God.**

Collect

Your ways are saving ways, O triune God. Teach us to ask what you as Jesus would do before we jump into action without considering what it means to honor you and to treat rightly those around us. In Jesus' name. Amen.

Prayer Of Confession

We, who carry our marveling at human creation to the extremes of conceit and pride, cannot compare ourselves to your wisdom and your power, O God. You are greater than an extension of ballooned human ego. Forgive us for making of ourselves foolish little gods. Amen.

22B Hymns

"On A Hill Far Away" Tune: THE OLD RUGGED CROSS
"Jesus, Keep Me Near The Cross" Tune: NEAR THE CROSS
"Lift High The Cross" Tune: CRUCIFIER

Third Sunday In Lent

Gospel: John 2:13-22
Theme: To The Point

Call To Worship
Jesus' turning over the tables of the money-changers in the temple reminds us of this truth: When you love something that you see is being disrespected, sometimes the only thing to do is defend it by being blunt, direct, and to the point.

Collect
Because we are your people, O God, we must not wait for you to do what we ourselves must do. We pray for the wisdom to discern ignorant meddling from deliberate advocacy. In the name of Christ. Amen.

Prayer Of Confession
God, let us keep our faith and all that we value from becoming debased or the object of disrespect. Help us to care enough about you to speak up and to act on behalf of what is important — even if we are strangers to such speech and action. For the sake of Christ. Amen.

22B Hymns
"Christ Loves The Church" Tune: HIGH STREET
"My Hope Is Built" Tune: MAGDALEN, MELITA or THE SOLID
    ROCK
"Grace Greater Than Our Sin" Tune: MOODY

Fourth Sunday In Lent

First Lesson: Numbers 21:4-9
Theme: I Will Pray For You

Call To Worship
When life's heartaches threaten to overtake us and we flail at whoever is handy, including our God, know that God will endure and that God's faithfulness will lift us up out of the muck.

Collect
Gracious God, with your guidance, we can be like Moses toward those who lash out at us because of their misery. Let us hear the ways in which the suffering ask us for help. Help us respond with prayer and right action. Amen.

Prayer Of Confession
Forgive us, God, for grumbling, complaining, and making a nuisance of ourselves when we should be appreciative of life itself. We push away from you, not realizing you are "for" us. In return, you do the opposite of what we expect, O forgiving Sustainer. You keep saving us, lifting us above our complaints, and giving us another chance at life because of your love for us. Thank you. Amen.

23B Hymns
"As Moses Raised The Serpent Up" Tune: MORNING SONG or "As Moses, Lost In Sinai's Wilderness" Tune: RIVER FOREST
"Love Lifted Me" Tune: SAFETY
"In The Cross Of Christ I Glory" Tune: RATHBUN

Fourth Sunday In Lent

Second Lesson: Ephesians 2:1-10
Theme: Amazing

Call To Worship

As much as we would like to take credit, the freeing of us for fullness of life and the saving of us from our own folly are not our own doing but the acts of a loving God. Come, let us dare to believe. Come into renewed life.

Collect

Amazed anew by your grace, O merciful God, we move from death of our souls to life in Christ. Changing us from children of wrath to children of love, God raises us to new life. By your grace, we too will come alive on Easter. Amen.

Prayer Of Confession

Turn our hearts around, O God, so we will be ready to let go of what separates us from ourselves, from others, and from you. Turn us around so we will be ready for resurrection. In the name of Jesus. Amen.

23B Hymns

"Amazing Grace" Tune: AMAZING GRACE
"Sovereign And Transforming Grace" Tune: MANTON
"Sunset To Sunrise Changes Now" Tune: KEDRON

Fourth Sunday In Lent

Gospel: John 3:14-21
Theme: Not Condemned

Call To Worship

Leader: "For God so loved the world that he gave his only Son so that everyone who believes in him may not perish but may have eternal life."

People: When we lose our way in life, God finds us.

Leader: "For God so loved the world that he gave his only Son, so that everyone who believes in him may not perish but may have eternal life."

People: When the spirit part of us becomes caged, God frees us.

All: "For God so loved the world that he gave his only Son, so that everyone who believes in him may not perish but may have eternal life." Thanks be to God.

Collect

Because of our belief, Gracious God, we may have eternal life. We do not earn it. We simply may have it as your gift. Thank you for sending Jesus into the world so the world might be saved through him. Amen.

Prayer Of Confession

Particularly during the inward looking that Lent invites, dear God, we focus upon what surely would condemn us. Yet you do not condemn us when we believe in you. Help us accept your taking to our long list of shortcomings the delete key of your freeing grace. Amen.

23B Hymns

"I Will Lift The Cloud Of Night" or "I Will Make The Darkness Light"
    Tune: JONES
"Love Lifted Me" Tune: SAFETY
"O Grant Us Light" Tune: HESPERUS

Fifth Sunday In Lent

First Lesson: Jeremiah 31:31-34
Theme: All Shall Know God

Call To Worship

Leader: God has promised, "I will be your God." God has promised, "You will be my people."
**People: These are the promises of God who sees us through all
our journeys, who is present as Spirit deep within us,
who will not desert us.**
Leader: Come, let us worship God.

Collect

As we come to know you within our hearts, O God, we show your
love in the way we act toward others. As we open our hearts to you
and discover that you are with us, our whole way of being changes.
We will be your people. Praise be to you, O God. Amen.

Prayer Of Confession

Many have given up the search for you, dear God, through empty,
traditional ways because we are looking from the outside, from the
external form, and on the surface. Teach us to be quiet and listen for
you with our whole being. Teach us the new way of knowing you
from within our hearts. Through Jesus. Amen.

24B Hymns

"God Reigns O'er All The Earth" or "This Is My Father's World"
    Tune: TERRA BEATA
"Glorious Is [Thy][Your] Name, O Jesus" Tune: GLORIOUS IS YOUR
    NAME
"There's A Wideness In God's Mercy" Tune: IN BABILONE

Fifth Sunday In Lent

Second Lesson: Hebrews 5:5-10
Theme: Reverent Submission

Call To Worship
One surprise of reverent submission to God lies in not losing one's identity but rather in finding one's true self. Come, follow the ways of God. Come, let us worship God.

Collect
Teach us your way, O God. Remind us that however confusing and disturbing life may become, you are on our side. We come to you with patience, determined to bear whatever suffering we must. For the sake of Christ. Amen.

Prayer Of Confession
We would rather use a different word for submission, O God. We do not like ideas of surrender, yielding, or giving in. Submission reminds us of our loss. Help us see the gain of reverent submission which places us within the realm of your plans. The obedience of reverent submission speaks of a welcoming acceptance that unites us with you. For the sake of Jesus. Amen.

24B Hymns
"Beautiful [Jesus][Savior]" or "Fairest Lord Jesus" Tune: SCHÖNSTER HERR JESU

"Be Still, My Soul" Tune: FINLANDIA

"Teach Me, My God And King" or "Teach Me, O Lord, Your Holy Way" or "Teach Me Thy Way, O Lord" Tune: ROCKINGHAM or MORNINGTON

Fifth Sunday In Lent

Gospel: John 12:20-33
Theme: Glory, Glory

Call To Worship
All earth all around us comes to life. All nature resounds. The season for last year's seed appears to have ended; yet its shell provides nourishment for the growth of the new plant. Last autumn's leaf fall breaks down and down into usable nutrients that give energy to this spring's leaf crop. The whole natural world prepares for life.

Collect
We get caught in particular births and deaths, O God, and forget the cyclical flow within a single moment — holding at once a unity of all that is, has ever been, and will be. In the dying of your Son, Holy Parent, lay the seed of life eternal so that all might know you. Amen.

Prayer Of Confession
We begin to see, O Sustainer, that Jesus' life and death transcend history. Let us see that the fruit of his life confirms truths measured beyond minutes and hours. Help us also to live not for ourselves alone but to nurture the vitality of those around us and offer sustenance for those yet to come. In the name of Christ. Amen.

24B Hymns
"My Song Is Love Unknown" Tune: RHOSYMEDRE
"[O][Our] God, Our Help In Ages Past" Tune: ST. ANNE
"[Mine][My] Eyes Have Seen The Glory" Tune: BATTLE HYMN

Sunday Of The Passion (Sixth Sunday In Lent)

First Lesson: Isaiah 50:4-9a
Theme: The Tongue Of A Teacher

Call To Worship

Know that God is a supportive, listening God who cares about our smallest needs. Know that God hears us and knows how to sustain us. Come, let us worship.

Collect

Teach us your way of caring, O God, so we might become good listeners and encouragers of those who would speak to us. Teach us when to be silent. Guide our responses toward a helpful manner when we are the confronted ones. Amen.

Prayer Of Confession

Many conversations begin with a moan of complaint, dear God. Help us to hear the plea of a weary person for a sustaining word and to avoid answering with our own litany of grievances. Help us to respond with the tongue of a teacher, to speak an encouraging word. In the name of Jesus. Amen.

25B Hymns

"Come, Teach Us, Spirit of Our God" Tune: MURRAY
"Teach Me, My God And King" or "Teach Me, O Lord, Your Holy Way" or "Teach Me Thy Way, O Lord" Tune: ROCKINGHAM or MORNINGTON
"Unto The Hills We Lift Our Longing Eyes" Tune: SANDON

Sunday Of The Passion (Sixth Sunday In Lent)

Second Lesson: Philippians 2:5-11
Theme: Empty

Call To Worship
Self-aggrandizement, thoughts of defining his legacy, enhancing his reputation, an air of self-importance — all these I-centered attitudes were absent from Jesus the day of Jesus' ride through Jerusalem. Laying aside any wishes for himself, Jesus emptied himself on this day of fullness. God lifted him up. Those who followed him gave him majesty and hosannas. Come, let us sing our hosannas to the Savior.

Collect
Teach us in a quiet manner to live the truth that we are your children, O holy Parent. Let us leave any glorifying to you. Amen.

Prayer Of Confession
We become so busy conveying an image of ourselves in our work, to our children, or to our friends, Gracious God, that we forget the telling of our story comes best from the perception of others. Help us to lay aside our own agendas for the sake of bettering the world around us and to let our story tell itself. For the sake of Jesus. Amen.

25B Hymns
"Hosanna, Loud Hosanna" Tune: ELLACOMBE
"Tell Me The [Stories][Story] Of Jesus" Tune: STORIES
"O Love, How Vast, How Flowing Free" or "O Love, How Deep, How Broad, How High" Tune: DEO GRACIAS **OR** "O The Deep, Deep Love Of Jesus" Tune: BUNESSAN or EBENEZER

Sunday Of The Passion (Sixth Sunday In Lent)

Gospel: Mark 14:1—15:47 or Mark 15:1-39 (40-47)
Theme: Temporary

Call To Worship
On the final Sunday in Lent, we consider the price of Jesus' sacrifice. Let us ponder what we have to offer as well as the ways in which we honor and give tribute to God and to those who are special in our lives.

Collect
The woman who anointed Jesus with the expensive ointment of fragrant nard reminds us not to wait too long to honor those whom you give us temporarily, O God. With investments of long-term loans, college bills, and mortgages on our minds, we scrimp and overlook the significance of a here-and-now gift. Help us discern when an act is more important than its cost. Amen.

Prayer Of Confession
In these days of wanting immediate gratification, we confuse the wasted luxury of living too much for the moment with a well-timed extravagance. Teach us, O God, to weigh the moment so we might discern when the time is appropriate for spending what we can ill afford. Amen.

25B Hymns
"Ride On! Ride On In Majesty" Tune: ST. DROSTANE, THE KING'S MAJESTY, or WINCHESTER NEW
"A Woman Came Who Did Not Count The Cost" Tune: WEXFORD CAROL
"All Glory, Laud, And Honor" Tune: ST. THEODULPH

Holy/Maundy Thursday

First Lesson: Exodus 12:1-4 (5-10) 11-14
Theme: I Will Pass Over You

Call To Worship
We look for signs that God will provide for our well-being. On Maundy Thursday we remember in the sharing of Holy Communion the holy meal of the first designated Jewish Passover — so filled with meaning that it was to mark the first month of the year.

Collect
In the quietness and community of this time together, our thoughts turn to sacrifice and to new beginnings. Each time we remember the Savior, we begin life anew. Each time we remember the sacrifice, we start afresh. Because of Jesus. Amen.

Prayer Of Confession
Seeing that you are faithful to your promises and covenants, O God, we will do our part by taking the time to remember and acknowledge the presence, caring, and sacrifice you have made on our behalf. We ask for guidance in our journey of faithfulness. Amen.

26B Hymns
"Here, O My Lord, I See [Thee][You] Face To Face" Tune: LANGRAN
"The King Of Love My Shepherd Is" Tune: DOMINUS REGIT ME
    or ST. COLUMBA
"According To [Thy][Your] Gracious Word" Tune: BANGOR or
    MARTYRDOM

Holy/Maundy Thursday

Second Lesson: 1 Corinthians 11:23-26
Theme: As Often As You Eat

Call To Worship

Jesus chose not something his disciples did once a year or once a month for remembering him. Jesus chose the main meal of the day, the evening meal after the day's work was finished. He chose not a delicacy seldom eaten or a special beverage that might be unavailable. He chose the basics — the bread and the juice of the vine. He wanted to be that close to his disciples and he wanted them to be that close to him. Come, sit at the table with your friends.

Collect

In sitting at the holy table, we join the community of other believers. In eating the holy meal, we sense union with the community of believers at once spanning all time and all places. Thank you, O gracious Host, for the invitation to sit at this table. In the name of Jesus. Amen.

Prayer Of Confession

We live so fast, dear God. What if we were to remember you each time we took nourishment? Our remembering need not be showy or long. It need not shape itself into words. It could be as easy a greeting to you as a pause of breath. But help us remember you, O God, so we also might give thanks. In the name of Jesus. Amen.

26B Hymns

"When I Survey The Wondrous Cross" Tune: HAMBURG or
    ROCKINGHAM OLD
"Let Us Break Bread Together" Tune: LET US BREAK BREAD
"It Was A Sad And Solemn Night" Tune: BOURBON

Holy/Maundy Thursday

Gospel: John 13:1-17, 31b-35
Theme: Later You Will Understand

Call To Worship

Understanding is not always the common denominator of human bonds. Sharing another's life through an act of caring draws us close and helps us transcend uncertainty while we await understanding. Come to Christ's table this Holy Maundy Thursday to share in the breaking of bread.

Collect

Grieving God, we open our hearts to meet you in your grief with our acts of kindness to others. Open our own graciousness to receive the thoughtful acts of others. In the spirit of Jesus. Amen.

Prayer Of Confession

We become so filled with wanting to do the right thing, O God, that we forget about the simple acts of showing our concern that mean so much to those who hurt. Keep open the eyes of our heart so we might notice the aching of those closest to us and be present for them in loving ways, as was our Savior for the disciples. Amen.

26B Hymns

"Jesu, Jesu, Fill Us With Your Love" Tune: CHEREPONI
"When Mary Bathed Our Savior's Feet" Tune: RUTH or ST. FLAVIAN
"Where Charity And Love Prevail" Tune: CHRISTIAN LOVE or ST. PETER

Good Friday

First Lesson: Isaiah 52:13—53:12
Theme: By A Perversion Of Justice

Call To Worship

Leader: He was wounded for our transgressions.
People: By a perversion of justice he was taken away.
Leader: He was crushed for our iniquities.
People: By a perversion of justice he was taken away.
Leader: Upon him was the punishment that made us whole.
People: By a perversion of justice he was taken away.
Leader: By his bruises we are healed.
All: By a perversion of justice he was taken away.

Collect

We stand with you today at the cross, O God, aware of how slowly
— even accidentally — the important changes happen in our world.
We stand with you committed to do our part to practice love by reliev-
ing misery where we find it. For the sake of your Son. Amen.

Confession

Forgive us, O merciful God, when we misuse justice. Forgive us
when we take the easy way out by using another as a scapegoat. Forgive us for going astray and turning to our own way when we could
have taken responsibility for what needed to be remedied. Forgive us,
O God, for killing you so many times. Amen.

27B Hymns

"O For A World" Tune: AZMON
"To Mock Your Reign, O Dearest Lord" Tune: KINGSFOLD
"We Shall Overcome" Tune: WE SHALL OVERCOME

Good Friday

Second Lesson: Hebrews 10:16-35
Theme: Where There Is Forgiveness

Call To Worship

Leader: Where there is forgiveness,
People: There is no need for more sacrifice.
Leader: Where there is forgiveness,
People: There is hope.
Leader: Where there is forgiveness,
People: There is a new and living way.

Collect

God of the cross, may we reflect the freeing, forgiving events of Good Friday by living thankful lives and by encouraging others to know the way of respect and concern for those around them. Amen.

Confession

Help us let this day of sacrifice for our sakes make a difference in our lives. Teach us, O God of compassion, to live within a circle of hope that permeates and influences all that we think and choose and do. Let us carry a perspective of hope into the classroom, the work-place, and the family kitchen. Amen.

27B Hymns

"Beneath The Cross Of Jesus" Tune: ST. CHRISTOPHER
"God Of The Sparrow, God Of The Whale" Tune: ROEDER
"I Am Thine, O Lord" Tune: I AM THINE

Good Friday

Gospel: John 18:1—19:42
Theme: "Judge Him According To Your Law"

Call To Worship
Today is the day we are in the depths. Before Easter could happen, Jesus had to endure the suffering of Good Friday. Let us stand here on this day with Jesus in the depths of grief.

Collect
How could you let this happen to your own son, God? We can hardly stand it that you let him die for our sake. We comprehend so little about sacrifice. We understand so little about the depth of your love. We know only about how it feels to lose someone we love. Amen.

Confession
Forgive us, God, when we play politics at the expense of others. Forgive us when we lack the mettle to stand for what is right and what is just. Forgive us for hating Pilate before we recognize that we are as human as Pilate. Amen.

27B Hymns
"Out Of The Depths I Call" Tune: ST. BRIDE **OR** "Out Of The Depths, O God, We Call" Tune: FENNVILLE

"What Wondrous Love Is This" Tune: CHRISTOPHER or WONDROUS LOVE

"How Could A God Whose Name Is Love" Tune: KINGSFOLD or TALLIS' THIRD TUNE

Easter (Resurrection Of Our Lord)

First Lesson: Acts 10:34-43
Theme: God Raised Him

Call To Worship

Leader: God is in charge. God raised Jesus. This is Easter.
People: God, who is the savior of all, accepts us and brings us hope through Easter.
All: **All praise to God. Christ our Savior is risen today.**

Collect

On this day, O triumphant Savior, hope becomes more than hype. More than an extravagant claim, hope becomes a new way of meeting each day. Thank you, God, for the gift of hope. Through Jesus the Christ. Amen.

Prayer Of Confession

As independent and self-directing as we are, O God, we must wait the long wait for you to raise us. It may not be today. Today, we may be quiet under burdens and only mouth the hymns of joy. While we wait for hope to defeat hopelessness, let the message and spirit of the Easter hymns seep in and begin the turnaround of our souls. Through Christ. Amen.

28B Hymns[1]

"Come, [Ye][You] Faithful, Raise The Strain" Tune: AVE VIRGO VIRGINUM, GAUDEAMUS PARITER, or ST. KEVIN
"Christ The Lord Is Risen Today" Tune: EASTER HYMN
"Joyful, Joyful, We Adore Thee" Tune: HYMN TO JOY

Easter (Resurrection Of Our Lord)

Second Lesson: 1 Corinthians 15:1-11
Theme: And

Call To Worship
Leader: Christ died for our sins, and . . .
People: He was buried
Leader: And . . .
People: He was raised on the third day
Leader: And . . .
People: He appeared to the disciples and beyond that
Leader: And . . .
People: He appears to you and to me.
All: And, we say praise to our risen Savior!

Collect
Not only did you die for our sins, Jesus, but you also were buried and raised on the third day. Then you carefully made sure that those who followed you saw that you had risen and recognized you. And to us today who believe in you, O Christ, you also find ways of making your presence known. We believe. We rejoice. Praise be to you, O Christ. Amen.

Prayer Of Confession
Your coming as the Resurrected Christ was long ago, O God, and yet Easter comes anew today. Renew our faith so we might live as people of faith. Strengthen our belief so it might radiate your presence for others. Refill our reservoirs of hope so we might persevere. Through Jesus the Christ. Amen.

28B Hymns[1]
"He Lives" or "I Serve A Risen Savior" Tune: ACKLEY
"I Come To The Garden Alone" Tune: GARDEN
"Up From The Grave He Arose" Tune: CHRIST AROSE

Easter (Resurrection Of Our Lord)

Gospel: Mark 16:1-8
Theme: Do Not Be Alarmed

Call To Worship

Leader: Today is the day to sing.
People: Christ is risen!
Leader: The great surprise, the empty tomb.
People: Christ is risen!
Leader: From now on, all is different. Today is Easter Day.
All: Jesus Christ is risen today!

Collect

We come to the tomb, like the women, prepared to do the one expected task, then find everything changed forever. Guide us, O God, as we also struggle to sort out amazement from fear and discover rejoicing. For Christ is risen. Amen.

Prayer Of Confession

Our heads are in such a muddle at times, O God, that we run from the tomb like Salome and the two Marys. We fail to comprehend. We do not believe or cannot believe what we see. So new is the idea of Easter entering our lives that approaching the tomb with hope does not occur to us. Open our hearts to belief as you opened the door of the tomb. Amen.

28B Hymns[1]

"Jesus Christ Is Risen Today" Tune: LLANFAIR
"O Sons And Daughters, Let Us Sing" Tune: O FILII ET FILIAE
"From All That Dwell Below The Skies" Tune: LASST UNS
    ERFREUEN or OLD HUNDREDTH

---

1. Try verse 3 of "Praise To God" Tune: SAKURA (NCH) as a congregational introit or before the pastoral prayer during the Easter season.

Second Sunday Of Easter

First Lesson: Acts 4:32-35
Theme: Partners

Call To Worship

Leader: Partners in concern,
People: Partners in planning,
Leader: Partners in doing,
People: Partners in giving,
Leader: Partners in sharing the load.
All: Christians are people in relationship. We strive to be of one heart and one soul. Come, let us worship God together.

Collect

We acknowledge that as your people, O God, we must live beyond ourselves. We recognize that as your people, we can combine skills and talents to help carry the burdens of those around us. Strengthen our response to your call to practice the art of sharing. Through Christ. Amen.

Prayer Of Confession

We need to be partners in Christ's service, gracious God, because none of us has enough strength to meet every need alone. The ongoing challenges wear us down. Teach us to share responsibilities and be your church together. In the name of Christ. Amen.

29B Hymns[1]

"Praise, My Soul, The King Of Heaven" **OR** "Praise With Joy The World's Creator" Tune: LAUDA ANIMA

"Called As Partners In Christ's Service" Tune: BEECHER

"Jesus Lives! The Victory's Won" Tune: JESUS, MEINE ZUVERSICHT

Second Sunday Of Easter

Second Lesson: 1 John 1:1—2:2
Theme: We Declare

Call To Worship

Leader: As did the disciples, let us declare together:
All: **What was from the beginning,**
What we have heard,
What we have seen with our eyes,
What we have touched with our hands,
What we know in our hearts to be true:
Leader: The eternal life that was with God and was revealed to us at Easter shows we have an advocate in God.
All: **Let us declare these things together and share the spirit of community.**

Collect

To you, who has proclaimed to us and who has announced and who has trumpeted as spring's resurrection trumpets — to you, we declare that we have heard in our innermost hearts the truth that has been part of your plan for us from the beginning, the life and the eternal life you have given us. We hear you and say to you, alleluia and amen.

Prayer Of Confession

We say thanks to you, O God, by our choice to heed the life wish rather than the death wish. We say thanks by our determination to respond rather than to ignore. We say thanks by opting to be people of compassion rather than of harshness. For the sake of the living Christ. Amen.

29B Hymns[1]

"Holy, Holy, Holy" Tune: NICAEA
"How Can I Say Thanks" Tune: MY TRIBUTE or "How Can I Thank You, Lord" Tune: O GOTT, DU FROMMER GOTT
"Father, We Praise [Thee][You], Now The Night Is Over" or "Rising In The Darkness" Tune: CHRISTE SANCTORUM

Second Sunday Of Easter

Gospel: John 20:19-31
Theme: Just Receive

Call To Worship
Lay aside your doubting and receive the Holy Spirit. Lay aside your wondering, lay aside your rational explanations, lay aside your speculation, and come. Receive the promise your Holy Parent has given you.

Collect
Thank you, O God, for knowing what we need before we can allow ourselves to make the choice of belief. Thank you for coming to us. Thank you for accepting our individuality. Amen.

Prayer Of Confession
When we meet you alone, O God, without the supportive nudges of those we trust, we think we, like Thomas, need something more to go on than simple faith. Bless us with your blessing that we who have not seen might come to believe. In the name of Jesus the Christ. Amen.

29B Hymns[1]
"Thine [Be][Is] The Glory" Tune: JUDAS MACCABEUS
"Joy Dawned Again On Easter Day" Tune: PUER NOBIS NASCITUR
"Savio[u]r, Like A Shepherd Lead Us" Tune: BRADBURY

---

1. As a closing response throughout the Season of Easter, sing verse one of "The Strife Is O'er" Tune: VICTORY.

Third Sunday Of Easter

First Lesson: Acts 3:12-19
Theme: So, Anyway

Call To Worship
So anyway, God says to us. So anyway, you can forget about the destructive stuff you have done. Just repent and turn to God so that your sins may be wiped out. So anyway, says our forgiving God, who sacrificed his son, the risen Christ, so that we might know fullness of life.

Collect
We worship you, O God, who has the power to heal, to forgive the sinner, and to inspire our faith. We cherish your approval of us as your created beings. We continually fall short yet glean from your acceptance the energy to try to live the best lives we can. In the name of Christ. Amen.

Prayer Of Confession
You amaze us, O God. We fail ourselves, we disappoint others, and we let you down. Still, you witness the ways we live that have had disastrous effects on others and on ourselves, and you choose to love rather than to destroy us. You seek no revenge for our killing Jesus daily by the way we live. Help us to accept ourselves, to accept each other, and to change our ways so they might more closely approximate your hopes for us. In the name of Christ. Amen.

30B Hymns
"The God Of Abraham Praise" Tune: LEONI or YIGDAL
"Shepherd Of My Soul, You Fulfill My Need" Tune: SOUL SHEPHERD
"Help Us Accept Each Other" Tune: AURELIA

Third Sunday Of Easter

Second Lesson: 1 John 3:1-7
Theme: God's Kids Hope

Call To Worship
When a parent says, "You are my child," it makes little difference whether that child is a birth-child, an adopted child, a foster child, or a neighbor child. The messages come through that the child is loved and the nurturer has hope for that child's future. From love, hope is born. As children of God, we are loved by God. God has hope for our future.

Collect
Like those in the youth of their lives, we come to you, O God, with a young hope and a new faith still to mature in the reflection of your love. Through the promise of Easter, we walk with you. Amen.

Prayer Of Confession
In the midst of the complexities and ambiguities of life, we glimpse evidence of your care, O sustaining Creator. Help us to keep open the eyes of our hearts so we might keep a healthy balance between what is reality and what we hope for. In the strength of your care. Amen.

30B Hymns
"Lift Up Your Hearts, Ye People" Tune: DU MEINE SELE, SINGE
   or GREENLAND
"Hail, Thou Once Despised Jesus" Tune: IN BABILONE
"The Whole Bright World Rejoices Now" Tune: HILARITER

Third Sunday Of Easter

Gospel: Luke 24:36b-48
Theme: Alive, I Say

Call To Worship
Alive, we say. You are alive, O Christ. Let us rejoice and let our hearts sing as resurrection truth swells. Come and worship God.

Collect
We, who need you not to leave us to ourselves, welcome any sign of your presence, O living Christ. We, who need you to guide us along our way, let the surging of song leap from our hearts. You live. All praise to you, O ever-present, living God. Amen.

Prayer Of Confession
Jesus, of all the evidence you gave the disciples that you live, it was your asking what there is to eat, like the first thing a child says after walking in the door, that brought you close to us. We need the tangible, the food, something a living person would do. We want to be convinced for our sake and for your sake, O Christ. Amen.

30B Hymns
"Christ Is Alive" Tune: TRURO
"You Gave My Heart New Songs of Praise" Tune: AZMON, NEW SONG, or WINCHESTER OLD
"Good Christian [Friends][Men] Rejoice And Sing!" Tune: GELOBT SEI GOTT

Fourth Sunday Of Easter

First Lesson: Acts 4:5-12
Theme: By The Name Of Jesus

Call To Worship

Leader: What if Christ were to become the cornerstone of the personal relationships we build?

People: What if Christ were the cornerstone of our money-spending decisions?

Leader: What if Christ were the cornerstone of the way we use our time?

People: What if we were to let Christ make a difference day by day in our lives?

All: What if we lived in the name of Jesus?

Collect

O living Christ, you are the hope of all that we do and are. Continue to show us how you would have us be and what you would have us do in your name. Amen.

Prayer Of Confession

Gracious, ever-building Creator, everyday activities distract us from our noble goals. Sometimes we have all we can do to keep present buildings from falling apart. Bolster our determination to keep Christ as the cornerstone of all our life. When we let go of your hope, cheer us on to pick it up again. Amen.

31B Hymns

"Hope Of The World" Tune: ANCIENT OF DAYS or DONNE SECOURS

"O Master Workman Of The Race" Tune: KINGSFOLD

"We Would Be Building" Tune: FINLANDIA

Fourth Sunday Of Easter

Second Lesson: 1 John 3:16-24
Theme: For One Another

Call To Worship

Leader: Let us show God's love by loving each other.
People: Respect those who differ from us as also loved by God.
Leader: Love one another.
People: Take time to greet others with a wave, a nod, a smile, a few words.
Leader: Love one another.
People: Share minutes listening with lonely persons of all ages.
Leader: Love one another.
People: Show consideration toward our families and those we meet at school, work, and through our activities.
All: Let us demonstrate God's love by loving one another.

Collect

As we practice living your love by loving others, you, O God, return that love to us many times over. You show us again and again how variously love makes itself known. Thank you for your gift of tenderness, O God. Amen.

Prayer Of Confession

If we are to honor the commandment to love one another, first we must stretch our thoughts beyond ourselves. This is hard, God, because we have little enough time to attend our own needs. Remind us that there is enough love to go around. Help us reserve both necessary energy for ourselves and energy for loving others in truth and action. In the name of Christ. Amen.

31B Hymns

"Love Divine, All Loves Excelling" Tune: BEECHER
"Spirit, Spirit Of Gentleness" Tune: SPIRIT
"In Christ There Is No East Or West" Tune: McKEE or ST. PETER
    OR "Where Charity And Love Prevail" Tune: CHRISTIAN LOVE, ST. FLAVIAN, or ST. PETER

Fourth Sunday Of Easter

Gospel: John 10:11-18
Theme: Hero

Call To Worship

Let us be as open-eyed children who enjoy the wonder-filled capacity to recognize a hero. Everyday heroes abound — a patient spouse, a courageous sibling, a valiant neighbor living with disease or handicap, workers who support their families by enduring disagreeable jobs, a teacher seeing hope in a stuttering student. Let us lift up the heroes of our day.

Collect

Today's collect will literally be a collected prayer. Consider for a moment someone whom you presently admire or have respected during your lifetime. Turning to your pew neighbor, speak the name of the person you have remembered. Tell briefly why you consider that individual to be a hero.

Prayer: Gracious and surprising God, you have heard the names of those we consider heroes. Bless these people with your blessing. Encircle them always with the gentleness of your caring. We ask in the name of Jesus the Christ. Amen.

Prayer Of Confession

Dear God, help us to care as deeply for each other as a shepherd cares for the sheep. When we become aware of someone in trouble, give us the courage to respond with our first impulse to help rather than letting second thoughts turn us away. Amen.

31B Hymns

"How Gentle God's Commands" Tune: DENNIS
"My Shepherd Is The Living God" Tune: CONSOLATION
"Such Perfect Love My Shepherd Shows" Tune: DOMINUS REGIT
    ME

Fifth Sunday Of Easter

First Lesson: Acts 8:26-40
Theme: Tell Me

Call To Worship
Do you always understand what you are reading when you read the Bible? This is the story of real people. The stories of the Bible are also about you and me. Come, let us listen to Holy Scripture with the ear of the heart as well as that of our hearing. Come, let us worship God.

Collect
Gracious God, through the stories of the Bible you tell us that you understand our situation, that we are not alone, and that whatever our circumstances, nothing can prevent us from being acceptable to you. We are grateful. Amen.

Prayer Of Confession
Open the ear of the heart, O God, so we, like the disciple Philip, will become aware of how others might recognize themselves in particular passages of Scripture. Let us listen for teachable moments rather than rushing ahead before another person is ready to hear the story. Then, let us tell the story of Jesus as clearly as we are able through our actions and our words. We pray in Jesus' name. Amen.

32B Hymns
"I Love To Tell The Story" Tune: HANKEY
"This Little Light Of Mine" Tune: LATTIMER
"You Are Called To Tell The Story" Tune: JULION

Fifth Sunday Of Easter

Second Lesson: 1 John 4:7-21
Theme: Brothers And Sisters

Call To Worship

Leader: I call you brother or sister because we share a parent.

People: I call you brother or sister because we have talked soul to soul with each other.

Leader: I call you brother or sister because we both live with cancer or broken relationships or memories of abuse.

People: I call you brother or sister because you are my neighbor.

All: We are brothers and sisters because we profess the same Christ and acknowledge that God is God.

Collect

We love because God loved us first. Because of your love, O compassionate One, let us recognize that all who are born of God are our brothers and sisters. Let your love be the holy connector among us. In the name of Christ. Amen.

Prayer Of Confession

We do not give you a chance to live, O God, unless we love one another. Help our love to be more than love in theory. Strengthen our love so we can extend it to the brothers and sisters who are hard to love. Help us recognize the negative energy of envy, avarice, jealousy, rivalry, and selfishness so we might better replace them with the power of a loving spirit. For the sake of Christ. Amen.

32B Hymns

"The Church's One Foundation" Tune: AURELIA

"Lord, We Thank Thee For Our Brothers" or "Thank Our God For Sisters, Brothers" Tune: PLEADING SAVIOR

"Sacred The Body" Tune: TENDERNESS

Fifth Sunday Of Easter

Gospel: John 15:1-8
Theme: Spring Pruning

Call To Worship
Spring pruning looks drastic. Sometimes it is. The result is equally surprising as double growth bursts forth from each cut and results in a better plant. Be warned, however, to make judicious pruning choices lest the thinning severs the main stem from which all sustenance arises.

Collect
We are here, O God, because we recognize you are the vine. The health of our spirit hinges on a strong relationship with you. Renew us with a right spirit, O God. Amen.

Prayer Of Confession
God of growing things, we want to grow, too. Keen our minds to pay attention to that about ourselves which is nonproductive so we might cull weakness from our lives and begin to thrive again. For the sake of Christ. Amen.

32B Hymns
"God Of Grace And God Of Glory" Tune: CWM RHONDDA
"Many Are The Lightbeams" Tune: LIGHTBEAMS
"Christ For The World We Sing" Tune: ITALIAN HYMN

Sixth Sunday Of Easter

First Lesson: Acts 10:44-48
Theme: Upon All

Call To Worship
The Holy Spirit falls upon all who hear the word. Ours is an inclusive faith. God as Holy Spirit enters our lives as freely and completely as God once came in the lively form of a human infant.

Collect
Your gift of the Holy Spirit, O gracious God, excludes no one who becomes aware of your presence — not the most liberal or most conservative church in town, not the unchurched person who hears only a hint of your whisper, not the disenchanted or too busy, not the person with alternative lifestyle or unfamiliar name or different skin tone. Your gift of the Holy Spirit comes to all. All praise to you, O God. Amen.

Prayer Of Confession
Dear God, help us to see more clearly whom we call Gentiles in our time. Help us to follow your lead and be as big-hearted as you. You come even to the Gentile within ourselves that we would rather not claim. Help us to grow through your all-encompassing love. In the name of the Holy Spirit. Amen.

33B Hymns
"God [Himself] Is [Present][Truly] With Us" Tune: WUNDERBARER KÖNIG
"Like The Murmur Of The Dove's Song" Tune: BRIDEGROOM
"Come [Forth][Down], O Love Divine" Tune: DOWN AMPNEY

Sixth Sunday Of Easter

Second Lesson: 1 John 5:1-6
Theme: No Burden Here

Call To Worship
Within the realm of loving God and honoring and respecting each other, God's commandments cease to threaten us or to cause us burden. Rather, they become serious yet gentle guides born from the Spirit of a God who is good.

Collect
We come into your presence as the people of God. We come as believers in you, O God, our Creator, Savior, and Sustainer. Amen.

Prayer Of Confession
The Holy Spirit is a mystery to us, O God. Still, we are aware of something that happens in how we treat others as you draw us toward extending our faith beyond ourselves. We see your commandments from another bearing. We confess our belief in the truth of the Spirit. Amen.

33B Hymns
"Let The Whole Creation Cry" Tune: SALZBURG
"How Gentle God's Commands" Tune: DENNIS
"Now In The Days Of Youth" Tune: DIADEMATA

Sixth Sunday Of Easter

Gospel: John 15:9-17
Theme: Friend

Call To Worship

Leader: Friendship is a relationship of trust and respect, of commitment and loyalty.
People: Friends are chosen, sharing, and open.
Leader: Friends have confidence in each other.
All: Let us be friends to one another.

Collect

Teach us, O God, to love each other as Jesus loved those he met. Amen.

Prayer Of Confession

It is difficult at first, dear God, for us to picture the relationship you hold with us as one of friendship. Then we realize friendship is an intimate and apt expression of your love through Jesus. You laid down your life for us. Help us live up to the responsibilities of friendship with each other and with you so we might live within the realm of your love. In the name of Christ. Amen.

33B Hymns

"Angels Holy, High, And Lowly" Tune: LLANHERNE
"[Jesu][Jesus], Priceless Treasure" Tune: JESU, MEINE FREUDE
"[Ye][You] Servants Of God" Tune: HANOVER

Ascension Of Our Lord

First Lessons: Acts 1:1-11
Theme: Restore The Kingdom?

Call To Worship
The disciples were not the only ones to ask Christ when the kingdom would be restored. Whenever you and I feel desperate, we ask the bottom-line question, "When, God?" When will people ever live together peaceably? When, God, will human misery around the world ever diminish? Not how, but when, God?

Collect
The strength of your power, O Spirit God, comes to us in ways we cannot fathom. What we do know is you will not leave us empty-handed. For this we are grateful. Amen.

Prayer of Confession
In a waiting time before a Pentecost in our lives we, like the disciples at the ascension of Christ, feel ill-equipped to manage alone in a broken world. Help us, O sustaining God, to hear Jesus' words that your realm offers a new way of meeting life. Help us to hear his promise that you will send what we need for empowerment. Amen.

34B Hymns
"The Voice Of God Is Calling" Tune: MEIRIONYDID
"Behold A Broken World" Tune: MARSH CHAPEL
"For The Healing Of The Nations" Tune: CWM RHONDDA

Ascension Of Our Lord

Second Lesson: Ephesians 1:15-23
Theme: Called To Hope

Call To Worship
God calls us from despair into a powerful hope which the eternal presence of Jesus Christ undergirds. Our task is to discern how this hope to which God calls us will shape itself. Come, let us worship the God of hope.

Collect
We trust you, O God, to bring a sturdiness and a steadiness to our plans. Grant us a spirit of wisdom as you reveal your hope for our world. Amen.

Prayer Of Confession
We want to repair what is broken immediately, O God. We forget that the unfolding of your plan for us takes time. Help us to be patient and discerning as we shape this hope into a form that will make a difference. Through the Spirit of Christ. Amen.

34B Hymns
"My Hope Is Built On Nothing Less" Tune: MELITA or SOLID ROCK
"Open My Eyes" Tune: OPEN MY EYES
"All My Hope [On God Is][Is Firmly] Founded" Tune: MICHAEL

Ascension Of Our Lord

Gospel: Luke 24:44-53
Theme: Thus It Is Written

Call To Worship
When we preface our words with "Thus it is written," we assert a connection with a strength and a base from the past. Thus it is written: What is happening now is grounded in something that has gone before. Thus it is written: As today's events unfold, they illuminate what first puzzled us. So it was at the time of ascension that Jesus drew to the attention of his disciples the writings of earlier scripture with these words: "Thus it is written."

Collect
We come to you, O God, carrying the puzzles of our lives and of the world around us, trusting that you will open us to see how everything fits together. For the sake of Jesus Christ. Amen.

Prayer Of Confession
Sometimes, God, when we experience acute isolation, we overlook elements of history that would help us gain perspective and find a fuller sense of meaning. Challenge us to view and treasure our lives as part of your greater plan. In the name of Christ. Amen.

34B Hymns
"We've A Story To Tell To The Nations" Tune: MESSAGE
"Great Is [Thy][Your] Faithfulness" Tune: FAITHFULNESS
"Glorious Things Of [Thee][You] Are Spoken" Tune: AUSTRIAN HYMN

Seventh Sunday Of Easter

First Lesson: Acts 1:15-17, 21-26
Theme: Replacement

Call To Worship

What if you had been called to replace one of Jesus' disciples? What if you were called to a position of responsibility in our church at a critical, uncertain time? What if the future of your work, your company, or your career depended upon your being ready to stand up for what you believe in when you are chosen?

Collect

We would be faithful, O God. We would take the risks of faith. We would live out what we believe because you have been faithful to your promises to us. In the name of Christ. Amen.

Prayer Of Confession

God, many of the important things we are called upon to do appear to happen by chance. Yet when we look more closely, we see that you have been preparing us all along. To you and to those who influence the choice, we are seen as faithful, as knowing what is happening, and as ready to shoulder the task. Help us to see for ourselves our strengths. For the sake of Christ. Amen.

35B Hymns

"I Sing The Mighty Power Of God" Tune: ELLACOMBE
"Come, Let Us Join With Faithful Souls" or "The Savior Calls; Let Every Ear" Tune: AZMON **OR** "For the Faithful Who Have Answered" Tune: OMNI DIE
"Stand Up, Stand Up For Jesus" Tune: WEBB

Seventh Sunday Of Easter

Second Lesson: 1 John 5:9-13
Theme: Son Of God

Call To Worship
Listen to these distant, external words about giving testimony: Give evidence, make a statement about, declare, speak as witness, give documentation, make a deposition.

Now hear these interior, personal words about testimony: "God gave us eternal life, and this life is in his Son. Whoever has the Son has life; whoever does not have the Son of God does not have life." Come in the name of the Son of God to worship the God who gave us eternal life.

Collect
We who believe in the Son of God have all the testimony we need within our hearts. We come to you, O God, not to be convinced but to profess our belief. All glory be to you, O life-giving God. Amen.

Prayer Of Confession
Sometimes, God, we look in the wrong places for evidence to convince us of the truth. We ask for the courage to trust the innermost voice of the heart. You sent us Jesus for a reason. You sent us the life of the Son of God so we might know you and your ongoing concern for us, your treasured creation. Help us to believe. In the name of Jesus the Christ. Amen.

35B Hymns
"The Head That Once Was Crowned With Thorns" Tune: ST. MAGNUS

"God Of Our Life" Tune: SANDON

"All Glory Be To God On High" Tune: ALLEIN GOTT IN DER HÖH

Seventh Sunday Of Easter

Gospel: John 17:6-19
Theme: We Are One

Call To Worship

Leader: One of the hardest moments we can know is the giving back of what has become precious. It was given temporarily in holy trust. However, it is time to move on when the task is complete.

People: **We know about letting go of our children. We know about turning over to someone else a project into which we have put our whole selves. We know about retiring from a career we have loved. We know about moving on beyond this earthly life. We know about uncertainty.**

All: **The ascension of Christ is about letting go, trusting and entrusting, and appreciating that we are all one.**

Collect

We remember, O God, that you are in charge. Before our time, you were guiding. You are present to lead us now. You will continue to guide us, rejoicing, into the future. Through the Holy Spirit. Amen.

Prayer of Confession

During times of change, dear God, our confidence temporarily fades. Uncertainty and grief make our inner world spin. Help us especially during these times to be aware of your strength, the courage and ability of those around us, and the resilience you have given us for moving into the future. Be with us, we pray. Amen.

35B Hymns

"Remember God Was Guiding" Tune: WEBB

"Community Of Christ" Tune: LEONI

"[They'll Know We Are Christians][We Are One in the Spirit]" Tune: ST. BRENDAN'S **OR** "Come, Let Us Join With Faithful Souls" Tune: AZMON

The Day Of Pentecost

First Lesson: Ezekiel 37:1-14 (Alternate)
Theme: You Shall Live

Call To Worship

Leader: Sometimes we find ourselves set down in the middle of a valley filled with dry bones.

Men: Our ideas have turned to dust.

Women: Our marketable attributes have shriveled.

Leader: Then something takes hold of this hopelessness and turns it around.

Men: A new idea fascinates us. We begin again to thrive.

Women: We recognize valuable talents that take us in a new direction.

All: The very spirit of life reconnects within us.

Leader: Is this not also the spirit of Pentecost? Is this not God active in our lives as Holy Spirit? Is this not God-with-us-always?

Collect

Whether we sit down surrounded by dried-out bones or step among them, you are with us, O God, bringing us to reality, staying with us, and meeting our inner conversation with these words, "You shall live." You breathe vitality into our very being. We are alive again. All praise to you, O living, ever-creating God. Amen.

Prayer Of Confession

Those times we become so disjointed within ourselves and so disconnected with those around us that all vitality drains from us, bring us to reality, O God. Spirit of God, descend upon our hearts. You, alone, know whether we can live fully. Tell us in ways we can hear that with you in our lives, our dry bones can know new life. Amen.

36B Hymns

"Spirit Of The Living God" Tune: LIVING GOD
"Spirit Of God, Descend Upon My Heart" Tune: MORECAMBE
"Every Time I Feel The Spirit" Tune: AFRICAN-AMERICAN SPIRITUAL

111

The Day Of Pentecost

Second Lesson: Romans 8:22-27
Theme: Like A Deep Sigh

Call To Worship

On Pentecost, God came blowing as the rushing wind of Holy Spirit into the hearts of Jesus' disciples. Like a sigh too deep for words, God comes as Holy Spirit whispering hope into our amazed and waiting hearts. Come into the presence of God.

Collect

We need not be concerned about framing perfectly worded prayers to you, O God, for you know the direction of our hearts. A stumbled few words, a change of posture, an acknowledgement within the soul — you know when we are at prayer and ready to listen and hope. Amen.

Prayer Of Confession

There are times, God, when all we can do is hope patiently. We know well our weaknesses of body and spirit. We come with a sigh too deep for words to you, O gracious One, and you, who searches our heart, meet it with your own deep sigh. And we cease to be alone with our patient hoping. Thank you, Holy Spirit. Amen.

36B Hymns

"Come, O Spirit, With Your Sound" Tune: BOUNDLESS MERCY or ST. KEVIN

"Let Every Christian Pray" Tune: LAUDES DOMINI

"I'm Goin'a Sing When The Spirit Says Sing" Tune: I'M GOIN'A SING

The Day Of Pentecost

Gospel: John 15:26-27; 16:4b-15
Theme: Are You Here, God?

Call To Worship
Come into the presence of God. Know that God is. Cherish our capacity to move beyond concepts of God that limit or diminish the Creator. Embrace the gift of the Holy Spirit sent to us. Let us worship God in spirit and in truth.

Collect
We do not always recognize you, God, as we grow beyond our earlier ideas about you. Then, there you are, more deeply present in Spirit than possible in human form. We praise you, ever-changing, ever-the-same, eternal, present Creator. Amen.

Prayer Of Confession
Leader: Are you here, God,
People: In the limbo of indecision and uncertainty?
Leader: Are you here, God,
People: In the changes when we feel completely on our own?
Leader: Are you here, God,
People: In the scary in-between times when we most need you to champion our efforts?
Leader: Are you here, God, when we need you?

36B Hymns
"Come, O Spirit, Dwell Among Us" Tune: EBENEZER
"O Come And Dwell In Me" Tune: ST. MICHAEL
"Surely The Presence Of The Lord" Tune: WOLFE

113

The Holy Trinity

First Lesson: Isaiah 6:1-8
Theme: Whoa!

Call To Worship
A throne, seraphs, a live coal touched to the mouth of the prophet Isaiah to cleanse his lips from sin? Whoa, you say. What on earth does Isaiah's curious vision have to do with me? Hear the bottom line. Isaiah did not take off in the opposite direction when encountering God. Rather, he stayed, listened to God's question, and answered, "Here I am. Send me." How does God gain your attention? Have you the courage to say, "I'll go on a mission for you, God"?

Collect
Here we are, O holy One, who comes to us as Creator, Savior, and Sustainer. We are listening as your Spirit speaks in equally novel ways to each of us. Grant us the boldness to be ready and to come forward with a "Yes!" Amen.

Prayer Of Confession
Triune God, who sometimes meets us in such strange manners that we, too, say, "I am lost," give us the courage to recognize you and respond to you with honesty so our conversations might continue. Amen.

37B Hymns
"Holy, Holy, Holy" Tune: NICAEA

"Every Time I Feel The Spirit" Tune: AFRICAN-AMERICAN or PENTECOST

"Lord, Dismiss Us With [Thy][Your] Blessing" Tune: REGENT SQUARE or SICILIAN MARINERS

The Holy Trinity

Second Lesson: Romans 8:12-17
Theme: Spirit Of Adoption

Call To Worship
Enthusiasm, readiness, eagerness, patience, longing, hope — this is the spirit of pre-adoptive parents awaiting their chosen, already loved child. So also is the spirit of adoption within the Holy Parent. Come into the family of God as approved, adopted children of God. Let us praise God together.

Collect
In the name of the Parent, the Son, and the Holy Spirit, we come to you and pray to you, O God. We come willing from our innermost hearts to acknowledge that we are yours so that we might leave behind all fear. We come willing to be led by the Holy Spirit so that we might lead others. For your sake. Amen.

Prayer Of Confession
Be the guardian of our hearts through the presence of your Holy Spirit. Be the champion of our plans through your Spirit. Be the defender of our decisions, O triune God. Amen.

37B Hymns
"Holy God, We Praise Thy Name" Tune: GROSSER GOTT, WIR LOBEN DICH

"We All Believe In One True God" Tune: WIR GLAUBEN ALL' AN EINEN GOTT

"Holy, Holy, God Of Glory" or "God The Spirit, Guide, And Guardian" Tune: HYFRYDOL

The Holy Trinity

Gospel: John 3:1-17
Theme: New

Call To Worship

Leader: The whole reason God sent Jesus into the world is so we, his creation, might be saved.

People: What are we saved from?

Leader: Ourselves, eternal chaos, all that separates us from God and from right relationships with those around us.

People: What are we saved for?

Leader: New life, new beginnings, new paths, the newness love brings.

Collect

We come to you on this day of new beginnings. We trust to you, O Holy Spirit, our rebirth from above. Come to us so we might know newness of life. Amen.

Prayer Of Confession

You said whoever believes, God. We, like Nicodemus, wonder how anyone can be born after having grown old. The habits we detest are as much a part of us as the way we walk. We have greeted the new day in the same manner for a lifetime. We meet change with our own typical responses. How can we be born anew with all these encumbrances? Dare we with so little understanding turn our hearts over to your holy Spirit? Amen.

37B Hymns

"Come, [Now][O][Thou] Almighty King" Tune: ITALIAN HYMN
"This Is A Day Of New Beginnings" Tune: BEGINNINGS
"All Creatures Of Our God And King" Tune: LASST UNS ERFREUEN

Corpus Christi

First Lesson: Exodus 24:3-8
Theme: Covenant

Call To Worship
Our gathering as God's people on this day is one way we show fidelity to the covenants we share with God. Particularly on the day of Corpus Christi, we remember the historical context of the blood of sacrifice that arose from the time of Moses.

Collect
We gather, O God, so that you might continue to reveal to us the truths of how we are to live within the responsibility of covenant. Open our hearts and minds as we strive to shape our lives within the framework of covenant. Amen.

Prayer Of Confession
It is a beautiful moment, O God, when your words of promise and our words of commitment meet in one voice. Let us renew the present-day symbols that help us seal and remember such holy moments. Amen.

38B Hymns
"Now Bless The God Of Israel" Tune: FOREST GREEN
"Thy Word Is A Lamp" Tune: THY WORD
"Word Of God, Come Down On Earth" Tune: LIEBSTER JESU

Corpus Christi

Second Lesson: Hebrews 9:11-15
Theme: His Own Blood

Call To Worship
In Christ, we live as free, reconciled people. Come and worship the living God as the people of God who are redeemed because of the singular, final sacrifice of Christ.

Collect
We lay aside works that are dead and fruitless unless we first acknowledge that the death of Jesus Christ has made all the difference for us. Amen.

Prayer Of Confession
When we get caught up in empty business and yearn again for fullness of life, O gracious Sustainer, help us to remember that the things we do are not to impress you but are offerings in response to what you first did for us. Through Christ. Amen.

38B Hymns
"Let All Mortal Flesh Keep Silence" Tune: PICARDY
"Be Known To Us In Breaking Bread" Tune: ST. FLAVIAN
"Jesus Took The Bread" Tune: NEW HOPE

Corpus Christi

Gospel: Mark 14:12-16, 22-26
Theme: Arrangements

Call To Worship
Having taken time to make ready for the holy meal, come into the presence of God with an inner quietness.

Collect
We leave outside the door what would distract us from being ready to share in your holy meal, O God. Amen.

Prayer Of Confession
Help us to make the proper arrangements within our hearts, dear God, so we will be prepared and spiritually present to share the holy meal at the appointed time. For the sake of Jesus the Christ. Amen.

38B Hymns
"Christ At Table There With Friends" Tune: MAUNDY THURSDAY
"Here, O My Lord, I See [Thee][You] Face To Face" Tune: ADORO
TE, LANGRAN, MORECAMBE, or PENITENTIA
"Take Time To Be Holy" Tune: HOLINESS

Proper 4
Sunday between May 29 and June 4 inclusive

First Lesson: 1 Samuel 3:1-20
Theme: Calling Your Name?

Call To Worship
Leader: Who is calling your name?
People: Things to buy, stuff and gadgets.
Leader: Drugs, empty foods, wasteful activities.
People: Television ads, throw-away technology.
Leader: Money greed. People who always want something from you.

Leader: Who is calling your name?
People: Enduring relationships, a purpose in life, meaningful work.
Leader: Spirit of God deep within, conscience, higher principles.
All: Can I hear? Am I listening?

Collect
You bring us change when you call us in the night, O God. We do not want to sleep through your call. Guide us so we may respond to you in a trustworthy manner. Amen.

Prayer Of Confession
God, who invites us to stretch our souls, you call our name in direction-choosing times. Help us to discern your call from all the other babble clamoring for our time, money, and energy. Lead us toward wholehearted responses that reflect faithfulness to your hopes for us. Amen.

39B Hymns[1]
"If [Thou][You] But Suffer God To Guide [Thee][You] Tune: NEUMARK

"Hush, Hush, Somebody's Calling My Name" Tune: AFRICAN-AMERICAN SPIRITUAL

"God Of Change And Glory [Many Gifts, One Spirit]" Tune: KATHERINE

Proper 4
Sunday between May 29 and June 4 inclusive

Second Lesson: 2 Corinthians 4:5-12
Theme: Green Leaves

Call To Worship
Even now the shadow of autumn leaves colors the summertime of trees. Occasional tips of deepening color hint of death yet green vitality governs its life-giving design. Come, let us begin worship together.

Collect
Leader: We are afflicted in every way,
People: but not crushed;
Leader: perplexed,
People: but not driven to despair;
Leader: persecuted,
People: but not forsaken;
Leader: struck down,
People: but not destroyed.
Leader: So death is at work in us,
People: but life in you, O God,
All: because of our choice of faith, because of your presence in our lives. We praise you, O God. Amen.

Prayer Of Confession
Dear God, we need to keep a balance between what brings darkness into our lives and your light that persists in bursting through that darkness. Let us accept what draws us toward awareness of our mortality while seeing clearly that the life you give is also at work in us bringing us to fullness of life. Amen.

39B Hymns[1]
"Hush, Hush, Somebody's Calling My Name" Tune: AFRICAN-AMERICAN SPIRITUAL
"O God, As With A Potter's Hand" Tune: WINSTON-SALEM
"Steal Away" Tune: STEAL AWAY

Proper 4
Sunday between May 29 and June 4 inclusive

Gospel: Mark 2:23—3:6
Theme: It's The Law

Call To Worship
God calls us to live by a higher law. God calls us to attend to the rule of compassion. God calls us to take responsibility for bringing about changes in our community and within the world community that will help people live better lives. Come, let us answer this call as we assume an attitude of worship.

Collect
We would be tenderhearted toward others who suffer, O compassionate God. We would become hardhearted toward our own self-serving and that we find in others. We would serve you without becoming self-righteous. Amen.

Prayer Of Confession
We ask for courage, O God, to do what is right even when we suspect it will bring us trouble. Teach us to ignore the ease of following the status quo for the wrong reasons. Help us persist while knowing that some misuse the law for their own interests. As we make our decisions, lead us toward asking what Jesus would do. We pray in his name. Amen.

39B Hymns[1]
"I Sing The Praise Of Love Almighty" Tune: ST. PETERSBURG
"I've Got A Feeling" Tune: I'VE GOT A FEELING
"Be Not Dismayed" or "God Will Take Care Of You" Tune: MARTIN

---

1. As a closing response for the Sundays of June, sing verse 3 of "May The Sending One Defend You" Tune: ROLLINGBAY.

Proper 5
Sunday between June 5 and June 11 inclusive

First Lesson: 1 Samuel 8:4-20 (11:14-15)
Theme: Listen To Their Voice

Call To Worship

The words we say are important. However, the sound of the human voice conveys as much of a message as the words — sometimes contradicting, sometimes confirming it. We must talk and listen with the heart if we are to communicate. Come, now, and worship in this space, aware of the sounds around us and the presence of our listening and compassionate Sustainer.

Collect

We come here to you, O God, hoping to meet you and each other in meaningful ways. As did our Savior, let us speak clearly to one another and listen with kind, patient ears. Amen.

Prayer Of Confession

Sometimes we hear the words of a person, O God, but neglect to listen to the voice in all that is said. We are busy planning our response or weighing the expected words. We miss the tone of a voice, a hesitant or quickened rate, or the hint of emotion. Then, when the conversation concludes, we feel that our souls have not touched. Help us to be better listeners. Amen.

40B Hymns

"Rejoice, O People, In The Mounting Years" Tune: YORKSHIRE
"A Charge To Keep I Have" Tune: BOYLSTON
"The Voice Of God Is Calling" Tune: MEIRIONYDID

Proper 5
Sunday between June 5 and June 11 inclusive

Second Lesson: 2 Corinthians 4:13—5:1
Theme: Day By Day

Call To Worship
In a unique, day by day inversion, as our external being wilts our inner, spiritual self strengthens. Come to worship today heartened by trusting the security and care of a loving God.

Collect
We come to you, O God, with a growing, ever-deepening faith in your unchanging presence in this life and the next. Help us tuck away this sustaining truth so we might know its comfort during those times we must withstand the turmoil of bodily distress. Amen.

Prayer Of Confession
When daily afflictions of our outer nature threaten to overwhelm us and the day seems to stretch out forever, dear God, help us to remember that your Spirit is at work now to deepen our spiritual being. Remind us that we need live only today, even an hour at a time. Let us leave for tomorrow the needs of tomorrow. Through the Holy Spirit. Amen.

40B Hymns
"Renew Your Church" Tune: ALL IS WELL
"Day By Day" Tune: BLOTT EN DAG
"Where He Leads Me" Tune: NORRIS

Proper 5
Sunday between June 5 and June 11 inclusive

Gospel: Mark 3:20-35
Theme: Short Division

Call To Worship

We make our Christian faith more complex than it is. If we are to be the church, then we must stand together as one family. Division divides and weakens us. Unity multiplies our might. If we are to be one in the Spirit, then the spirit of the heart must join with the Holy Spirit. Come, let us worship as God's spirited, Spirit-filled people.

Collect

We are your church, O Holy Spirit. We would be single-hearted in following the principles you have set before us. We would be single-minded in shaping and realizing our plans for this church. For the sake of Jesus Christ. Amen.

Prayer Of Confession

Great God, we stand before you filled with contradictions, with "would be's" contrasted with reality, with expected richness of relationship sullied by human faults. Help us to keep reaching toward integrity of spirit and toward strength in unity with a minimum of compromising attitude. Amen.

40B Hymns

"We Are The Church" Tune: PORT JERVIS
"Trust And Obey" Tune: TRUST AND OBEY
"We Limit Not The Truth Of God" Tune: OLD 22ND or ELLACOMBE

Proper 6
Sunday between June 12 and June 18 inclusive

First Lesson: 1 Samuel 15:34—16:13
Theme: On The Heart

Call To Worship
We look on the outward appearance, but God looks on the heart. God sees beneath the facade to the beauty of the human soul. Come and worship here where we might shed gloss and pretense. Let us discover ourselves and others anew.

Collect
We enter peaceably into the depths of the soul, O gracious God, knowing that you move there in your mysterious way to renew our courage. You invite us to claim both the negative and positive sides of our heritage. You replace dread with smile and self-doubt with confidence. You show us who we are. In the name of Christ. Amen.

Prayer Of Confession
We wonder why our spiritual life flounders in the shallows. We make decisions based on the outward appearance of those who would be our associates, our friends, or companions. Then we wonder why these relationships fail to flourish. Help us to be brave, God, and risk showing our true selves to others as well as to ourselves. Amen.

41B Hymns
"Forward Through The Ages" Tune: ST. GERTRUDE
"Into My Heart" Tune: Response
"God Moves In A Mysterious Way" Tune: DUNDEE

Proper 6
Sunday between June 12 and June 18 inclusive

Second Lesson: 2 Corinthians 5:6-10 (11-13) 14-17
Theme: Wrapping Paper

Call To Worship
How do you look at others? When we see others from a human
point of view, we tend to become critics of failings and shortcomings.
When we view others from Christ's perspective, we see aspects of a
person worthy of boasting and deserving of hope. "So," says the apostle
Paul, "if anyone is in Christ, there is a new creation: everything old
has passed away; see, everything has become new!"

Collect
The miracle of confidence comes from you, O God. The love of
Christ urges us forward. The love of Christ opens for us a new cre-
ation. All praise to you, our triune God. Amen.

Prayer Of Confession
Dear God, we confess our yearning to be part of a new creation.
We tire of our old ways but want to be more than our old selves re-
packaged in fancy wrapping paper. May we take on the new life that
reflects being recipients of the love of Christ and that models through
and through the way of Christ's love. Amen.

41B Hymns
"Blessed Assurance" Tune: ASSURANCE
"We Are Not Our Own" Tune: YARNTON
"Incarnate God, Immortal Love" or "Strong Son Of God, Immortal
    Love" Tune: ROCKINGHAM

Proper 6
Sunday between June 12 and June 18 inclusive

Gospel: Mark 4:26-34
Theme: Small Packages

Call To Worship

Leader: We think we must do great things to change the world around us. Know that great changes come about because of our smallest efforts.

People: An appropriate word,

Leader: A few minutes of shared time,

People: A promise honored,

Leader: A moment of confident enthusiasm

People: Can spawn a fresh start.

Collect

Creator God, we recommit ourselves to the hope that your realm will win out in the struggle for justice and peace and engender fullness of life and vitality in our world community. Amen.

Prayer Of Confession

We underestimate the possibilities of each talent and ability you have given us. We undervalue how flexible and adaptable we are in shaping ideas that generate positive change around us. Teach us, O God, to cherish, use, and expand even the smallest seed of promise that you have given us. Through the Holy Spirit. Amen.

41B Hymns

"O How Glorious, Full Of Wonder" Tune: IN BABILONE

"We Plant A Grain Of Mustard Seed" Tune: NEW BEGINNINGS

"Take My [Gifts][Life]" Tune: MESSIAH, TALAVERA TERRACE, or VIENNA

Proper 7
Sunday between June 19 and June 25 inclusive

First Lesson: 1 Samuel 17:(1a, 4-11, 19-23) 32-49
Theme: The Lion's Paw

Call To Worship

Leader: Who is your Goliath?
**People: The welfare system, the wearing out of body and mind
that aging or disease brings, alcoholism, drug addiction,
a domineering spouse, unemployment, economic situation, all that seems impossible to overcome.**
Leader: What lion's paw have you dared to confront?
**People: Change, uncertainty, the unknown, the day to day,
attitudes, responsibility, all that we rather would not do
but do anyway.**
Leader: Who is your strength and your bulwark?
People: God is our strength. God is our security.

Collect

When we have deterred the lion's paw with your help, O God, we
know we will be brave enough to take on Goliath. Should we not
outwit Goliath, our try still will have been honorable in your sight.
Amen.

Prayer Of Confession

It is easy to turn away when a challenge first presents itself. It is
more difficult to ignore it when the lives of others are at stake, when
we sense our responsibility, and when we realize we alone are called
to the task. Bring to us the inner calm of knowing that you stand
beside us as we grapple with difficult situations. Amen.

42B Hymns

"A Mighty Fortress Is Our God" Tune: EIN' FESTE BURG
"Be [Calm][Still], My Soul" Tune: FINLANDIA
"I've Got Peace Like A River" Tune: PEACE LIKE A RIVER

Proper 7
Sunday between June 19 and June 25 inclusive

Second Lesson: 2 Corinthians 6:1-13
Theme: The Acceptable Time

Call To Worship

Leader: At the acceptable time, God helps us.
People: The Holy Spirit is the power that helps us to do right things.
Leader: At the acceptable time, God renews us.
People: The Holy Spirit is the power that helps us to be brave.
Leader: At the acceptable time, God restores us.
People: The Holy Spirit is the power that helps us to meet what our lives demand.
Leader: At the acceptable time, God saves us.
People: The Holy Spirit is the power that helps us to shape our lives in the image of God.
All: We praise God's holy name.

Collect

Our hearts are open to you, O guiding One. Show us the way, for we are listening to you. Through the power of the Holy Spirit. Amen.

Prayer Of Confession

We try as best we know to show you our faithfulness, O God. Help us to sort out what in our lives is service and what borders on manipulation. Through your Spirit, guide us toward decisions that reflect the promises we have made to you. Amen.

42B Hymns

"Father Almighty, Bless Us" Tune: INTEGER VITAE
"How Like A Gentle Spirit" Tune: SURSUM CORDA
"[We Are Often Tossed And Driven][We'll Understand It Better By And By]" Tune: BY AND BY

Proper 7
Sunday between June 19 and June 25 inclusive

Gospel: Mark 4:35-41
Theme: Deep Water

Call To Worship

Leader: God, do you not care when we are perishing?
People: Know that God cares when we are perishing. Peace, be still.
Leader: God, do you not notice when we are scared?
People: Know that God cares when we are afraid. Peace, be still.
Leader: God, do you not watch as we risk ourselves?
People: Know that God cares when we venture forth. Peace, be still.

Collect

Thou, who leads us through deep, turbulent water, we approach you with the hope of knowing another depth, that of the silence within our soul as we become aware of your presence. Amen.

Prayer Of Confession

We need you to be near always, O sustaining Creator, for much we cannot do on our own. Clear our ears of anxiety's rumble so we can hear you telling us, "Peace, be still." Amen.

42B Hymns

"I Need [Thee][You] Every Hour" Tune: NEED
"Jesus, Savior, Pilot Me" Tune: PILOT
"How Deep The Silence Of The Soul" Tune: TALLIS' THIRD TUNE

Proper 8
Sunday between June 26 and July 2 inclusive

First Lesson: 2 Samuel 1:1, 17-27
Theme: Lion Friendship

Call To Worship
Leader: By what qualities do we measure a friendship as strong as lions?
People: Persons who stand by each other during rough times.
Leader: Persons who can speak to each other without censor.
People: Persons who support each other as they undertake adventures.
Leader: Persons who are dependable, trustworthy, and loyal.
All: **Persons who accept each other for who they are.**

Collect
You, O God, who lifts the cloud of night in our lives, are as a friend to us. We are grateful that we can speak freely to you without sending you away. We are thankful that we can count on your relationship to us as enduring, and that you wish well for us. In the name of Jesus the Christ. Amen.

Prayer Of Confession
We limit our friendships, O God, when we neglect their give-and-take nature. When we focus on our own goals, we restrict the fullness of communion possible within a friendship. Help us to reach beyond ourselves as we grow deeper friendships. In the spirit of Christ. Amen.

43B Hymns
"There Is A Balm In Gilead" Tune: BALM
"As Pants The Hart For Cooling Streams" or "As The Hart Longs" Tune: MARTYRDOM or AVON
"I Will Lift The Cloud Of Night" Tune: JONES

Proper 8
Sunday between June 26 and July 2 inclusive

Second Lesson: 2 Corinthians 8:7-15
Theme: Slim Pickings

Call To Worship
God calls us to do our part by being givers according to the money,
things, and talents that we have. God is the source of encouragement
that empowers us to finish with enthusiasm what we have begun.

Collect
We want our ventures to reflect our desire to be better Christians.
We want to be more loving, more giving, and more like Jesus. Amen.

Prayer Of Confession
What can we do, O God, those times we sense the plethora of need
yet are caught in droopy enthusiasm? Help us accept that abundance
of spirit fluctuates and needs our patience just as our tangible resources
at times slip into a spell of slim pickings. Help us to continue stretch-
ing our soul, our talents, and our resources. If we are in earnest, what
we offer will be acceptable to you. For the sake of Jesus. Amen.

43B Hymns
"Lord, I Want To Be A Christian" Tune: I WANT TO BE A
    CHRISTIAN
"Breathe On Me, Breath Of God" Tune: TRENTHAM
"Awake, My Soul, Stretch Every Nerve" Tune: CHRISTMAS

Proper 8
Sunday between June 26 and July 2 inclusive

Gospel: Mark 5:21-43
Theme: Life Wish

Call To Worship

Leader: What is it about the life wish that leads us to do what we ordinarily would not or could not do?

People: Is it desperation or hope that brings us to the miracle of restoration?

Leader: Can we save ourselves, or must someone intercede for us?

People: Must we become partners with God in order to make it through life and to thrive?

Leader: We come with many questions because living life fully is our goal, but living fully is exacting.

Collect

You, O God, are the source of the life wish that wells within us. You empower us with the hope that we are worthy of life. Through the Holy Spirit. Amen.

Prayer Of Confession

We need the comfort and assurance of your leading us on, O God. We admit that we are weak, that we are weary and worn down by the pressures of daily living, from the frailties of body and spirit, and from asking ourselves to do less or more than we are able. Because our independence is not omnipotent, we need your help to come through the temporary times of feeling our vitality nearly depleted. Amen.

43B Hymns

"Tell Me The Stories Of Jesus" Tune: STORIES OF JESUS
"There Was Jesus By The Water" Tune: TALITHA CUM
"Precious Lord, Take My Hand" Tune: PRECIOUS LORD

Proper 9
Sunday between July 3 and July 9 inclusive

First Lesson: 2 Samuel 5:1-5, 9-10
Theme: Kin

Call To Worship
Remember that who we are is directly related to Whose we are. Remember that in the eye of God, we are all kin. God calls us to leadership and to sharing responsibility as members of the family of God. Come, let us worship our Creator. Amen.

Collect
To you, O God who gives us health, life, and livelihood, renews us, and sustains us, your family sings praise. Amen.

Prayer Of Confession
Surround us, O God, with people who remind us of who we are and Whose we are so we will understand more fully why we are set in certain life situations. For the sake of the family of God. Amen.

44B Hymns
"Sing Praise To God [Our Highest Good][Who Reigns Above]" Tune: MIT FREUDEN ZART
"O My Soul, Bless God, The Father" Tune: STUTTGART
"The King Of Love My Shepherd Is" Tune: DOMINUS REGIT ME or ST. COLUMBA

Proper 9
Sunday between July 3 and July 9 inclusive

Second Lesson: 2 Corinthians 12:2-10
Theme: A Reason

Call To Worship

Leader: Is it possible that human weaknesses are for a reason?
People: We believe in a God who wishes well for us.
Leader: Is it possible that hardships are to give us limits?
People: We believe in a God who not only shaped but also sustains us.
All: It is possible that in our weaknesses we find strength.

Collect

You continually re-introduce us to hope, O God, as you teach us to come to new understandings about our gifts of talent, personality, and inadequacy. Thank you for the capacity to grow. Through your Holy Spirit. Amen.

Prayer Of Confession

We know, God, that when we stop complaining about our weaknesses and cease mourning what we can no longer do, something tender begins to happen within us. We let our frailties awaken alternative ways of doing things. We find other ways to use our talents. We learn patience and hope because we become "can do" people again. The "I can't" keeps us realistic but no longer defeats us. Strengthen our tenacity, O God, so we might sing a new song of life to you. Amen.

44B Hymns

"Praise To The Lord, The Almighty" or "Sing Praise To God, Who Has Shaped" Tune: LOBE DEN HERREN

"You Gave My Heart New Songs Of Praise" Tune: AZMON, NEW SONG, or WINCHESTER OLD

"Have Faith In God" or "Lord Jesus, Think On Me" Tune: SOUTHWELL

Proper 9
Sunday between July 3 and July 9 inclusive

Gospel: Mark 6:1-13
Theme: Little Ado

Call To Worship
Human hope is more fragile than God's hope. Sometimes in particular situations, we are ineffective. Our talents and expertise appear worthless, wasted. Then, when human hope wilts, it is time to remember God's hope for us. Come, let us worship the God of hope.

Collect
Let your awareness of our value, O gracious One, be a contagious lure that invites us to rediscover our sense of worth and validity. Let your faith in us empower our fortitude and rekindle our daring. Amen.

Prayer Of Confession
Dear God, when we do our best but are not appreciated, help us to give up and let go and move on. Keep us from wasting more ado, spending costly energy, and standing in the way of those who might thrive in our place. Encourage us to continue growing in other ways. Amen.

44B Hymns
"He Leadeth Me" Tune: HE LEADETH ME
"God Is At Work In Life" Tune: WORKING
"Children Of The Heavenly Father" Tune: TRYGGARE KAN INGEN VARA

Proper 10
Sunday between July 10 and July 16 inclusive

First Lesson: 2 Samuel 6:1-5, 12b-19
Theme: Dance!

Call To Worship
Where does confidence come from? When King David moved the ark of God, he danced with all his might before God. He danced as suits one wearing a piece of linen clothing called an ephod. This vestment worn by priests was a symbol of religious authority. What inner or outer garment reminds you to dance your dance with all your might?

Collect
From writing and singing of psalms to playing the lyre and dancing to the tambourine, music was the art form of King David's life. We praise you, O God, with the unique art forms of our lives. We dance our dance for you with all our might. Amen.

Prayer Of Confession
We dance to perform. We dance to please. We dance to express our joy. We dance as a whole-body way to praise you, our God. Even in our sitting still, let our lives be a dance to you. Amen.

45B Hymns
"Joyful, Joyful, We Adore Thee" Tune: HYMN TO JOY
"Lift Every Voice And Sing" Tune: LIFT EVERY VOICE
"I Danced In The Morning" Tune: LORD OF THE DANCE

Proper 10
Sunday between July 10 and July 16 inclusive

Second Lesson: Ephesians 1:3-14
Theme: Forward

Call To Worship

Leader: We go forward
People: Because God has blessed us in Christ.
Leader: We go forward
People: Because God has chosen us to love.
Leader: We go forward
People: In the strength of the name of Christ.
Leader: We go forward
People: Freed for fullness of life.
All: All praise to God.

Collect

We come before you, O God of blessings, knowing we hold the responsibility for our actions and for living out our lives as fully and honorably as possible. We can triumph over that which would seduce and distract us because your blessings reveal we live not for ourselves alone. All praise to you, O God. Amen.

Prayer Of Confession

When we try to live without a "because," we flounder and hesitate and move backward. When we try to live within the focus of your "because," we flounder, hesitate, and move backward, then go forward again with renewed resolve. Keep us mindful of your "because" in our lives, O God. In the name of Jesus Christ. Amen.

45B Hymns

"Forth In [Thy][Your] Name I Go" Tune: DUKE STREET
"In [Thee][You] Is Gladness" Tune: IN DIR IST FREUDE
"Sent Forth By God's Blessing" Tune: THE ASH GROVE

Proper 10
Sunday between July 10 and July 16 inclusive

Gospel: Mark 6:14-29
Theme: In A Careless Moment

Call To Worship
Jealousy, misused power, the thwarting of another's plans, pointing out one's sin — all can lead to the politically wrong dance. By doing what they do to initiate change, advisers, counselors, guides, and leaders in all positions risk losing heads in scheming struggles for power.

Collect
We would dance the dance of leadership with integrity. We would hold to high values with tenacity. We would stay with what is right despite the risks. We need your support, O God. Amen.

Prayer Of Confession
As nations and as individuals, give us the strength, O mighty God, to choose between right and wrong, between what is moral and immoral, despite the times, vanity, and careless moments. For the sake of Christ. Amen.

45B Hymns
"[O][Our] God, Our Help In Ages Past" Tune: ST. ANNE
"For All [Thy][Your] Saints, O Lord" or "O Savior, For The Saints"
    Tune: FESTAL SONG
"Jesus, Still Lead On" Tune: SEELENBRÄUTIGAM

Proper 11
Sunday between July 17 and July 23 inclusive

First Lesson: 2 Samuel 7:1-14a
Theme: Planting People

Call To Worship

Leader: As the prophet Nathan said to King David, I say to you, "Go, do all that you have in mind; for the Lord is with you."
People: **Do you mean to carry out my life hope, to become grounded, to become planted in my own place?**
Leader: I mean, have plans and dare to pursue them because God is with you.
All: **We give thanks to God who knows our hopes and is with us.**

Collect

We remember, O God, that while we have hopes in mind, your presence and your promises to humankind encourage and sustain us. We are grateful. Amen.

Prayer Of Confession

When we move on in our lives, we sometimes think, dear God, that we have left you behind as we have left behind everything else. Everything in our lives has changed and yet you remain constant. Let us not become so busy, so tired, or so preoccupied that we fail to make a place for you in our lives. Strengthen our resolve to go ahead with what we have in mind because you still are with us. Through the Spirit of God. Amen.

46B Hymns

"God Of [Our Fathers][The Ages], Whose Almighty Hand" Tune: NATIONAL HYMN
"God, Whose Love Is Reigning O'er Us" Tune: LAUDA ANIMA
"May God Embrace Us With His Grace" Tune: ES WOLLE GOTT UNS GNÄDIG SEIN

Proper 11
Sunday between July 17 and July 23 inclusive

Second Lesson: Ephesians 2:11-22
Theme: Strangers To Promise

Call To Worship

Leader: We are without Christ when we are caught in the commotion of hostility.

People: We are without Christ when we refuse the love of others.

Leader: We are without Christ when we are so self-absorbed that we neglect loving others.

People: We are without Christ when we separate ourselves from others and become as strangers.

Collect

Compassionate Creator, we would be makers of friendship rather than hostility. We would be with Christ as those who unite. We would be with Christ as peacemakers. In his name. Amen.

Prayer Of Confession

Dear God, help us to become aware of the walls that divide us from each other at levels of family, city, county, state, country, and nation. Strengthen our determination to carry your promises into all levels of society. Amen.

46B Hymns

"Hope Of The World" Tune: ANCIENT OF DAYS or DONNES SECOURS

"[Jesu][Jesus], Priceless Treasure" Tune: JESU, MEINE FREUDE

"Peace I Leave With You, My Friends" Tune: PEACE, MY FRIENDS

Proper 11
Sunday between July 17 and July 23 inclusive

Gospel: Mark 6:30-34, 53-56
Theme: Give Me A Break

Call To Worship

Leader: "Come away to a deserted place all by yourselves and rest a while."

People: **We do so much coming and going that we have no leisure even to eat.**

Leader: "Come away to a deserted place all by yourselves and rest a while."

People: **We give and give and give until nothing is left of us to give.**

Leader: "Come away to a deserted place all by yourselves and rest a while."

Collect

Just the thought of a time-out, a pause and respite, brings us comfort, O God. Let us find during this service of worship a time to pause from ceaseless reaching out and a time to find renewal for the spirit. Amen.

Prayer Of Confession

Well, God, sometimes we feel drained from caring about others, from giving when there seems no more energy for loving, and from coming up with more ideas and new plans for accomplishing the goals we have set. Teach us not to berate ourselves for compassion exhaustion. Show us how to recognize and schedule spaces for self-care. Show us how to nourish our whole being. Show us how to gain the rest that rejuvenates the spirit and from which mental vitality springs. Amen.

46B Hymns

"Who Trusts In God A Strong Abode" Tune: BISHOPGARTH or WAS MEIN GOTT WILL

"Jesus' Hands Were Kind Hands" Tune: AU CLAIR DE LA LUNE

"Immortal Love, Forever Full" Tune: SERENITY

Proper 12
Sunday between July 24 and July 30 inclusive

First Lesson: 2 Samuel 11:1-15
Theme: Contradiction

Call To Worship
Let us be as constant as Uriah the Hittite in doing our work without letting distraction interfere. Let us dare to live with honor when those around us make lesser choices. Let us garner strength from God for the journey through our own human contradictions.

Collect
We look to you, O God, who has the power to keep us from wavering from our ideals. We ask you to awaken within us the desire and the choice to improve the way we live. For the sake of Christ. Amen.

Prayer Of Confession
We are filled with contradictions, God. We are less scrupulous than we could be. We put personal matters before work. We scheme at the expense of others and ourselves to cover up our flaws and improprieties. Forgive our unwise ways. Help us to live honorable lives. For the sake of Jesus. Amen.

47B Hymns
"[All][He] Who Would Valiant Be" Tune: MONKS GATE or ST. DUNSTAN
"Dear God, Embracing Humankind" or "Dear Lord And Father Of Mankind" Tune: REST
"What Does The Lord Require" Tune: SHARPTHORNE

Proper 12
Sunday between July 24 and July 30 inclusive

Second Lesson: Ephesians 3:14-21
Theme: Inner Strength

Call To Worship
Leader: God is at work within us, rooting and grounding us in love.
People: We sing in the strength of God.
Leader: Let us trust in God to equip us for each task.
People: We live in the strength of God.
All: Come, let us praise God.

Collect
God, who guides us so that we can greet whatever comes with inner strength, you anticipate our need with a ready presence. With your power at work in us, we can do more than we thought possible. We give you thanks, O God, for inner strength. Amen.

Prayer Of Confession
We are limited in our capacity to comprehend and know the breadth, the length, the height, and the depth of Christ's love. Teach us and show us your way, O God, so we might grow daily in the fullness of your love. Amen.

47B Hymns
"The Church's One Foundation" Tune: AURELIA
"You Are The Way; To You Alone" Tune: DUNDEE
"If [Thou][You] But Trust In God To Guide [Thee][You]" Tune: WER
   NUR DEN LIEBEN GOTT

Proper 12
Sunday between July 24 and July 30 inclusive

Gospel: John 6:1-21
Theme: Provide

Call To Worship
Mostly, you and I live in circumstances of quantity, of plenty, even of excess. Yet, how little it takes to satisfy when that offered is given from compassion. We recognize Jesus in the act. We appreciate further that God is a caring sustainer.

Collect
We give our praise to God, who provides for all our needs. We give our trust to God who finds a way not only to manage our needs but to bring contentment. Through Jesus Christ. Amen.

Prayer Of Confession
At times, O God, we are overwhelmed by the task at hand. We begin to consider ways of running away. Remind us to stay and to keep as a priority caring for others. Remind us to trust that you will provide for basic needs of body and spirit. Through the Savior, Jesus Christ. Amen.

47B Hymns
"Come, Let Us Join with Faithful Souls" or "The Savior Calls; Let Every Ear" Tune: AZMON

"Come, O Fount Of Every Blessing" Tune: NETTLETON

"Hymn Of Promise" or "In The Bulb There Is A Flower" Tune: PROMISE

Proper 13
Sunday between July 31 and August 6 inclusive

First Lesson: 2 Samuel 11:26—12:13a
Theme: Confront

Call To Worship

Leader: When we do inexcusable things that bring hurt to others, we deserve like treatment. However, when we face the truth, see ourselves as we really are, and regret our actions, God offers not an eye for an eye but forgiveness.

People: **No matter who we are, we are accountable for our actions. No matter who we are, when we accept responsibility for our failures, God forgives us and we are free to try again.**

Collect

We gather as imperfect people, O God, asking for the courage to see where we are failing to live as your loving people and for the valor to change our ways. Amen.

Prayer Of Confession

Can you forgive us, God, for living such faulty lives? We recognize and deplore the wrong things others do but fail to see that we are guilty of equal defects in caring. Confront us with the truth. Set our lives on a new track. For the sake of Christ. Amen.

48B Hymns[1]

"All People That On Earth Do Dwell" Tune: OLD HUNDREDTH
"Come [Down][Forth], O Love Divine" Tune: DOWN AMPNEY
"Take My Life, O Lord, Renew" Tune: PATMOS or "Take My Life And Let It Be" Tune: MESSIAH

Proper 13
Sunday between July 31 and August 6 inclusive

Second Lesson: Ephesians 4:1-16
Theme: Growing Up

Call To Worship
We are a church composed of an abundant mixture of people with many levels of spiritual maturity. Hear the challenge to be the church listening and speaking to each other in a manner that champions each of us and encourages a graceful way of being the church together.

Collect
In response to your generosity, O God, we hope to lead lives worthy of our calling. In reply to your calling for a sense of oneness in your church, we reach toward a goal of unity of faith. Through your Spirit. Amen.

Prayer Of Confession
We recognize, gracious God, that the maturing of our spiritual nature is an ongoing process of growth. We ask for courage and strength as we move from being vulnerable children in the faith toward adults who are able to speak the truth in love and to hear truth spoken in love. In the name of Christ. Amen.

48B Hymns[1]
"With The Lord Begin Your Task" Tune: FANG DEIN WERK
"We Thank You God For Prayer" Tune: BOYLSTON or TAFT STREET
"Let Me Be [Thine][Yours] Forever" Tune: LOB GOTT GETROST MIT SINGEN

Proper 13
Sunday between July 31 and August 6 inclusive

Gospel: John 6:24-35
Theme: Bread Of Life

Call To Worship
Jesus is the bread of life. Whoever comes to Jesus will no longer be hungry. Whoever believes in Christ will no longer be thirsty. Let us renew our faith in Christ, that the belly of the soul might be filled. Come, let us approach God with hopeful hearts.

Collect
Great Sustainer, who gives life to this world, who sees that we have food for the body, who opens the way to nourishing the spirit, we give you thanks. We receive your life-sustaining gifts as we receive your gift of Christ. Amen.

Prayer Of Confession
We become so engrossed in pursuing the work that supplies nourishment for the body that we neglect putting energy into finding spiritual food that endures. Encourage us, O God, to create spaces in our everyday work so we might quiet the gnawing in the soul. In the name of Christ. Amen.

48B Hymns[1]
"Come, Teach Us, Spirit of Our God" Tune: MURRAY
"O Holy Spirit, Enter In" Tune: WIE SCHÖN LEUCHTET
"God Reigns O'er All The Earth" or "This Is My Father's World"
    Tune: TERRA BEATA

---

1. For a closing response throughout August, sing verse 4 of "Have Faith In God" Tune: SOUTHWELL.

Proper 14
Sunday between August 7 and August 13 inclusive

First Lesson: 2 Samuel 18:5-9, 15, 31-33
Theme: Instead Of You

Call To Worship

"Would that I had died instead of you" — these words of grief from one left behind are particularly poignant cried by a parent. Today, let us embrace by prayer those we know who have lost an infant through miscarriage, stillbirth, or sudden infant death. Let us remember those who have lost a child, a youth, or an adult child. Receive the comfort of this congregation and the solace of God who walks with you throughout this long journey.

Collect

We lift up to you, O Comforter, those who grieve the loss of a child. We trust in your strength to guide and sustain. Through the care and love of the Holy Spirit. Amen.

Prayer Of Confession

Stay near to those who grieve, O God. Quiet involuntary feelings of guilt. Grant patience with the floods of reliving that rush in. Help a parent to tolerate the distress of regret with a minimum of energy wasted on bitterness. Strengthen the resolve to continue meaningful life. Bring the calm of peace. Amen.

49B Hymns

"From Depths Of Woe I Cry To You" or "Out Of The Depths" Tune: AUS TIEFER NOT

"In The Midst Of Life" Tune: MITTEN WIR IM LEBEN SIND **OR** "In The Midst Of New Dimensions" Tune: NEW DIMENSIONS

"Guide Me, Ever Great Redeemer" or "Guide Me, O [My][Thou] Great Jehovah" Tune: CWM RHONDDA[1]

[1.] Let the choir alternate verses of "For The Healing Of The Nations" Tune: CWM RHONDDA (NCH) with the congregational singing of "Guide Me."

Proper 14
Sunday between August 7 and August 13 inclusive

Second Lesson: Ephesians 4:25—5:2
Theme: No Room For Bitterness

Call To Worship

Leader: Here is the Apostle Paul's list for right relationships:
Women: Speak the truth.
Leader: Be angry but do not sin.
Women: Resolve your anger before sunset.
Leader: Do not make room for the devil.
Men: Give up stealing.
Leader   Let only talk useful for building up come out of your mouth.
**Men: Put away all bitterness, wrath, wrangling, slander, and
           malice.**
People: Be kind to one another.
Leader: Be tenderhearted.
People: Forgive one another.
All: Live in love as Christ loved us.

Collect

We are here, O God, because we want to lead better lives, engage
in clean, right relationships, and draw one another toward greater kindness. Let us be encouragers as we attempt to live in a Christian manner. Amen.

Prayer Of Confession

You tell us to put away from us all bitterness, God, because bitterness causes death of our spirit. We would prefer to keep an ounce of
bitterness to call up when we are in a foul mood, just to remind us that
we are human. Instead, increase our kindness, so we will let go of all
bitterness, putting it beyond our reach. For the sake of Christ's love.
Amen.

49B Hymns

"Out Of The Depths, O God, We Call" Tune: FENNVILLE
"Spirit, Open My Heart" Tune: WILD MOUNTAIN THEME
"From The Crush Of Wealth And Power" Tune: BRIDEGROOM

Proper 14
Sunday between August 7 and August 13 inclusive

Gospel: John 6:35, 41-51
Theme: Life Bread

Call To Worship

Leader: Life bread
People: Teaching by God
Leader: Life bread
People: Freeing for life
Leader: Holy Spirit nourishing with life bread
People: Holy mystery among us still.

Collect

Jesus Christ, the God-connection; Holy Spirit, the God-connection; Holy Creator-Parent-God, we come to you drawn by you and drawn to you, O Thou, offerer of life bread. Amen.

Prayer Of Confession

Holy Spirit, bread of life given for us, return us to the root of all life. Give to us energy of the spirit so we might be fully awake to healing, to things of the light, to overcoming loss, to remembering hope. Amen.

49B Hymns

"O Holy Spirit, Root Of Life" Tune: PUER NOBIS NASCITUR
"Eternal Spirit Of The Living Christ" Tune: ADORO TE DEVOTE
"Holy Spirit, Ever Dwelling" Tune: NETTLETON

Proper 15
Sunday between August 14 and August 20 inclusive

First Lesson: 1 Kings 2:10-12; 3:3-14
Theme: An Understanding Mind

Call To Worship
"Ask what I should give you," God invited young King Solomon in a dream. Solomon asked God to give him an understanding mind able to discern good from evil. What one thing would you ask God to give you? God also gave Solomon something he had not asked for. What unrequested gift do you suppose God might give you that you also need?

Collect
At your invitation, O God, we ponder what is most important to us. In your generosity, you give us support and encouragement beyond our requests. We come to you with hearts filled with gratitude. Amen.

Prayer Of Confession
In our haste, we may wish for or ask for the wrong things, Holy Parent. Help us to focus on cultivating the enduring qualities that will sustain us throughout our lives. Encourage us to trust that you will meet our needs. Amen.

50B Hymns
"Praise The Source Of Faith And Learning" Tune: PROCESSION
"Grant Us Wisdom To Perceive You" Tune: QUEM PASTORES
"Lord, Make Me More Holy" Tune: LORD, MAKE ME MORE HOLY

Proper 15
Sunday between August 14 and August 20 inclusive

Second Lesson: Ephesians 5:15-20
Theme: Spirit Of Wisdom

Call To Worship

Leader: We are responsible for how we live. We are the makers and managers of our decisions. Come, let us take care to live as wisely and with as great understanding as possible.

People: We give thanks to God for all that God gives us in the name of Jesus the Christ and through the Holy Spirit.

Collect

Hear our prayer, O spirit-living God, that your presence will come to us as wisdom and that our response to you will bring an inner song to our heart. Amen.

Prayer Of Confession

Dear God, we have already wasted more time than we want to admit. We pray not only for ourselves but particularly for the younger ones among us that they might gain early wisdom to realize that decisions made now will determine the physical, mental, and spiritual quality of their remaining life. Guide us all as wisdom, O God. Amen.

50B Hymns

"Come, Holy Spirit, Heavenly Dove" Tune: ST. AGNES

"Spirit Of The Living God" Tune: IVERSON

"Be [Now] [Thou] My Vision" or "Christ Be My Leader" Tune: SLANE

Proper 15
Sunday between August 14 and August 20 inclusive

Gospel: John 6:51-58
Theme: Unless

Call To Worship

Leader: Unless we eat the flesh of the Son of Man and drink his blood, we will have no life in us.

People: Unless we accept what Jesus offers us freely, we will have no lasting life within us.

Leader: Unless we recognize the sacrifice of life Jesus made for our well-being, we will be without the life of the spirit that endures.

People: When we take the spiritual nourishment that God provides through Christ, we gain eternal life.

Collect

Our physical and spiritual energy comes from you, O God. Jesus gave up his life so our world might become a better place. We would live as people who have taken on the life of Christ so we might bring positive, nourishing energy to the world around us. Amen.

Prayer Of Confession

Sometimes, O God, we only go through the motions of receiving the elements of holy communion. Let us see afresh that each time we drink the juice and eat the bread with faith you transform us, make us new, and remind us again of the eternal life of the spirit that is ours through your loving Spirit. Amen.

50B Hymns

"O The Depth Of Love Divine" Tune: STOOKEY

"Bread Of The World" Tune: EUCHARISTIC HYMN

"Deck Thyself, My Soul, With Gladness," "Deck Thyself With Love," or "Graced With Garments Of Great Gladness" Tune: SCHMÜCKE DICH

Proper 16
Sunday between August 21 and August 27 inclusive

First Lesson: 1 Kings 8:(1, 6, 10-11) 22-30, 41-43
Theme: No God Like God

Call To Worship
Leader: In no way can we box God's love within only the walls of our own presumptions.
People: No way.
Leader: In no way can we limit God's outstretched arm only to what is comfortable within our own circle.
People: No way.
Leader: In no way can we confine God's concern only to within the place of a church building.
People: No way.
Leader: God's promises are for everyone, everywhere, through all time.
All: Always. Alleluia. Amen.

Collect
We come to this place, O great God, for we know we will find you here. We find you in what is familiar to our circles. We find you within the walls of our individual boxes of identity. While you are greater than our smallness, you live also in our house. Thank you. Amen.

Prayer Of Confession
Dear God, we want to keep you special for ourselves. Help us to bring you into the houses of others. We want to envision you as you have always been. Help us to note your presence in new situations. We get stuck in our seasoned ways. Help us to recognize new forms emerging as a result of your faithfulness to us. Let us share you with all our heart. Amen.

51B Hymns
"Now Thank We All Our God" Tune: NUN DANKET
"Lord Of Glory, You Have Bought Us" Tune: HYFRYDOL
"O God Of All Your People Past" Tune: NUN FREUT EUCH

Proper 16
Sunday between August 21 and August 27 inclusive

Second Lesson: Ephesians 6:10-20
Theme: Cosmic Powers

Call To Worship

Leader: When we put on the whole armor of God, we can stand up against ominous and evil powers.

People: With God, we can stand firm against violence in school, in the workplace, on the highway.

Leader: In the strength of God, we can confront the greed that promotes poverty.

People: With God, we can move beyond the drought, earthquake, and tornado.

Leader: With the whole armor of God, we can overcome death of the soul.

Collect

The qualities of truth, peace, righteousness, faith, and salvation are your words, O God. Never out-of-date, let them remain our words, strengthening and fortifying us for living in these days. For the sake of Christ. Amen.

Prayer Of Confession

Remind us amidst discouragement, O God, that your power is stronger than the evil presence in our world. Remind us, O God, even though the wrong appears constant, that truth, peace, righteousness, and love provide us with sufficient strength for persisting in the struggle for what is right. In the name of Christ. Amen.

51B Hymns

"Before Jehovah's [Aweful][Awesome] Throne" Tune: OLD HUNDREDTH or PARK STREET

"Fight The Good Fight" Tune: GRACE CHURCH, GANANOQUE or PENTECOST **OR** "God Is My Strong Salvation" Tune: MEIN LEBEN

"Rejoice, O Pilgrim Throng" or "Rejoice, Ye Pure In Heart" Tune: MARION

Proper 16
Sunday between August 21 and August 27 inclusive

Gospel: John 6:56-69
Theme: What?

Call To Worship
God offers to all who believe what will sustain us and bring newness of life. Come, let us open our hearts to receive the truth God would have us know. Let us worship the God of life.

Collect
We come to you, O living God, knowing that we waver between belief and unbelief, between faith and no faith. We come to you wanting to take you into our lives. We want to receive nourishment and sustenance as rich as the food that builds and rebuilds the cells of our bodies. Be life to us, O God. Amen.

Prayer Of Confession
Some teachings just do not make any sense, God. We think we comprehend you, then realize we are trying to take your words literally and that is not what you meant at all. We become discouraged and move closer to disbelief. Your symbols and parables and metaphors are at once confusing yet clear as they point us toward truth. Move us toward better understanding so we will respond from spirit as well as from the head to your Holy Spirit. Amen.

51B Hymns
"Abide With Me" Tune: EVENTIDE
"God Of Wisdom, God Of Grace" Tune: ST. KEVIN
"Holy Spirit, Light Divine" Tune: SONG 13 or "Holy Spirit, Truth Divine" Tune: CANTERBURY

Proper 17
Sunday between August 28 and September 3 inclusive

First Lesson: Song of Solomon 2:8-13
Theme: Spring Fever

Call To Worship

Leader: When we are in love with life, the whole world has beauty.
People: **When morning has broken and the sun renews the day, the bird song in our hearts sings.**
Leader: When we chance to see wildlife or examine the perfection of an opening summer flower, how can we think of other than the benevolence of a loving God?
All: **Let us sing songs of praise and thanksgiving to God.**

Collect

We make time to love life, O God, because your love of life is a constant presence that surrounds us. We touch the petal of a Cosmos blossom or notice the head of a sunflower as it follows the sun's course. We love our lifemates and our children with all our hearts. We enjoy the beautiful form of the human body and rejoice in the infinite variety of your creation. Thank you. Amen.

Prayer Of Confession

Wake up our exuberance for life, Holy Creator. Open our eyes and our ears to recognize when the time of singing has come. Give us a good dose of spring fever in the middle of summer. Amen.

52B Hymns[1]

"Morning Has Broken" or "Praise And Thanksgiving" Tune: BUNESSAN
"Take My Life, [And Let It Be][O Lord, Renew]" Tune: PATMOS
"Praise To God" Tune: SAKURA

Proper 17
Sunday between August 28 and September 3 inclusive

Second Lesson: James 1:17-27
Theme: As First Fruits

Call To Worship
All good gifts around us are gifts from God who wishes us well. Like first fruits of old brought to God, let us live exemplary lives that are gifts of thanksgiving to God. Like first fruits produced when the plant is at fullest potency, let us spend our highest energy on best acts. Come, let us bring thankful selves to God.

Collect
We offer you our best, O generous Creator, by living decent, honorable lives. We offer you our best by choosing excellence over the mediocre, action above sloth, and an awareness of your presence in all that we do. Amen.

Prayer Of Confession
Help us be like first fruits among your creatures. Draw us away from wasting our talents on the trivial, lest we have no energy left over for creating what matters most. For the sake of Christ. Amen.

52B Hymns[1]
"We Plow The Fields And Scatter" Tune: WIR PFLÜGEN
"My Prayer Rises To Heaven" Tune: VIETNAM
"[I][We] Sing The [Almighty][Mighty] Power Of God" Tune: ELLACOMBE

Proper 17
Sunday between August 28 and September 3 inclusive

Gospel: Mark 7:1-8, 14-16, 21-23
Theme: From Within

Call To Worship

Leader: Let us be transformers in a broken world.
People: Rather than bringers of harm, we would be healers.
Leader: Let us be transformers in a broken world.
People: Rather than destroyers, we would be builders.
Leader: Let us be transformers in a broken world.
People: Rather than devising havoc, we would bring about wholeness.

Collect

We gather, O God, as people who want to be stronger Christians. We want our lives to make a positive impact on the world around us. We want to be more loving. We want to be like Jesus. Amen.

Prayer Of Confession

Bring us to the acknowledgement of the source of our actions, O God. Fortify us for taking responsibility for all we do without blaming our environment, heritage, or others. Come into our hearts so that good intentions may come from our hearts. For the sake of Christ. Amen.

52B Hymns[1]

"Behold A Broken World" Tune: MARSH CHAPEL
"Lord, I Want To Be A Christian" Tune: I WANT TO BE A CHRISTIAN
"Into My Heart" Tune: Response

---

1. Throughout the month, sing the refrain to "We Plow The Fields And Scatter" Tune: WIR PFLÜGEN as a closing response.

Proper 18
Sunday between September 4 and September 10 inclusive

First Lesson: Proverbs 22:1-2, 8-9, 22-23
Theme: All God's Children

Call To Worship
We are all God's children who deserve to live in peace and abundance. We are all God's partners whose skills and abilities can share the struggle to raise the level of compassion in the world. We are all one family called to lift up the crushed members of God's family.

Collect
We renew our covenant to work together as the people of your realm, O God, to make this world a better place. In the name of Jesus the Christ. Amen.

Prayer Of Confession
We prefer to hoard our belongings and to focus on matters of self-interest. Move your Spirit among us, O God, so we might notice and then protect those who cannot manage by themselves. We prefer to think we have little influence on world matters. Move your Spirit among us, O God, so we might become aware of the hurts of those close to us and resolve to help. In the name of Christ. Amen.

53B Hymns[1]
"Now Is The Time Approaching" Tune: WEBB
"We Cannot Own The Sunlit Sky" Tune: ENDLESS SONG
"Thou God Of All, Whose Spirit Moves" Tune: OLD 22ND

Proper 18
Sunday between September 4 and September 10 inclusive

Second Lesson: James 2:1-10 (11-13) 14-17
Theme: Work Clothes

Call To Worship

Leader: Faith wearing work clothes is alive.
People: So let our faith respond to the neighbor facing bankruptcy.
Leader: Faith wearing work clothes lives.
People: So let our faith respond to the associate who has been unable to find work after downsizing.
Leader: Faith wearing work clothes lives.
People: So let our faith respond to the mother who finally dares to leave an abusive spouse.
Leader: Faith wearing work clothes lives.
People: So let our faith respond to the elder who is considering suicide.
All: Let us put on the work clothes of our faith.

Collect

We gather together wearing fancy clothes and plain ones. We assemble with pockets of indebtedness and well-paying stocks. We come together as people rich with hope and of skimpy faith to do your work in this world. Amen.

Prayer Of Confession

Remind us to stretch beyond what is easy to do, O God. Remind us to put on the work clothes of our faith. Remind us to open our own spirit so we can reach beyond ourselves with unbiased caring. In the name of Jesus the Christ. Amen.

53B Hymns[1]

"In Christ There Is No East Or West" Tune: McKEE or ST. PETER
"Spirit Of Jesus, If I Love My Neighbor" Tune: BENJAMIN
"Jesus, With Thy Church Abide" Tune: VIENNA

Proper 18
Sunday between September 4 and September 10 inclusive

Gospel: Mark 7:24-37
Theme: Open Up To Life

Call To Worship

Leader: Open us to hear, O God.
People: Open us to see.
Leader: Open us to feel.
People: Open us to live.
All: Open us to do your work.

Collect

Even when we are in strange surroundings, among people different from ourselves, or in uncomfortable situations, we are still yours,
O God. We still want to do what is fair and what is right. In the name
of Jesus the Christ. Amen.

Prayer Of Confession

Even when we yearn to go about unrecognized or without social
responsibility, you, God, are there calling to us. Keep us open to the
life around us. Keep us open to finding ways in which we can make a
difference. Keep us open to your wisdom. Amen.

53B Hymns[1]

"Pass Me Not, O Gentle Savior" Tune: PASS ME NOT
"Pray For A World Where Ev'ry Child" Tune: CANONBURY or
    CHILDREN
"Christian, Rise And Act [Thy][Your] Creed" Tune: INNOCENTS

---

1. As a congregational introit throughout September, sing one verse of "Enter, Rejoice, And Come In" Tune: ENTER, REJOICE.

Proper 19
Sunday between September 11 and September 17 inclusive

First Lesson: Proverbs 1:20-33
Theme: Storm Shelter

Call To Worship
Consider the following provisions for a storm shelter for the spirit: willingness to listen for God, readiness to hear God, love of knowledge, an attitude of praise rather than of ridicule, openness to new and other ways of doing things, dedication to the truth.

Collect
We come, O God, with hearts open to discern what is true and what is wise, knowing that truth and wisdom come from you. Strengthen us for living within the freedom of your truth and your wisdom. Amen.

Prayer Of Confession
Wisdom is hard to come by, God. Our usual stubbornness, shortsighted self-interest, and arrogance are inadequate equipment for meeting the calamities that overwhelm us. We pray that you will continue to find ways to offer us counsel. Through the name of Jesus. Amen.

54B Hymns
"Open My Eyes, That I May See" Tune: OPEN MY EYES
"O God, O Lord Of Heaven And Earth" Tune: WITTENBERG NEW
"Dear Jesus, In Whose Life I See" or "Sun Of My Soul, O Savior Dear" Tune: HURSLEY

Proper 19
Sunday between September 11 and September 17 inclusive

Second Lesson: James 3:1-12
Theme: Watch Your Tongue

Call To Worship
Is your tongue a catalyst that motivates others to improve themselves? Is your tongue a teacher of important matters? Is your tongue a rudder for a fair and right course?

Collect
Let the words that come out of our mouths be acceptable to you, O God. Let our words reflect the wisdom we glean from gathering as your church and being your people. In the spirit of Christ. Amen.

Prayer Of Confession
Just as I am may not be good enough, O merciful God, yet we know we must come to you as we are before we can hope to change. Forgive us for the errors of tongue that have led to trouble. Forgive us for the letting go times when a few ill-chosen words inflame an insult. Hearten us so that we do not give up on ourselves. Amen.

54B Hymns
"Just As I Am" Tune: WOODWORTH
"Lord, Speak To Me" Tune: CANONBURY
"There's A Wideness In God's Mercy" Tune: WELLESLEY

Proper 19
Sunday between September 11 and September 17 inclusive

Gospel: Mark 8:27-38
Theme: You Missed The Mark, Peter

Call To Worship
You got it right, Peter, when you answered Jesus saying, "You are the Messiah," but you blundered, Peter, by scolding Jesus.

Collect
Strengthen us to face what we must face, O God, knowing that you will remain by our side. Bring to us those who will call us to the reality of what will happen and to the honesty of consequences. In the name of the Holy Spirit. Amen.

Prayer Of Confession
How often, O God, we start out right, then become self-protective when we hear truths we would rather not hear. Our humanness overrides our first response and we draw away from the agitation or refuse to take it seriously. Help us to get back on track before it is too late. Amen.

54B Hymns
"Before Your Cross, O Jesus" Tune: ST. CHRISTOPHER
"How Can I Say Thanks" Tune: MY TRIBUTE
" 'Take Up [Thy][Your] Cross,' The Savior Said" Tune: DEUS TUORUM MILITUM, GERMANY, or NUN LAST UNS DEN LEIB BEGRABEN

167

Proper 20
Sunday between September 18 and September 24 inclusive

First Lesson: Proverbs 31:10-31
Theme: Call Her Happy

Call To Worship
Let us greet each day with wisdom, kindness, and laughter. Let us recover the delight of being as fully well in mind, body, and spirit as possible so the quiet smile of peace will shape itself. Let us live out our days with strength, dignity, and tenacity.

Collect
Leader: Happy are we when we use our strength for wholehearted and responsible living.

People: Thank you, ever-growing God, for the times we know a sense of meaning and fulfillment.

Leader: Happy are we when we recognize, develop, and use our talents.

People: Thank you, O creative God, for the times we are productive.

Leader: Happy are we when we are able to communicate with those closest to us.

People: Thank you, O compassionate God, for the times we feel a sense of oneness and unity.

All: Amen.

Prayer Of Confession
We are imperfect, God. We expect too much. We hope for too little. Give us the patience to keep trying and the faith to allow things to happen bit by bit. Our prayer is to bring those nearest to us more good than harm, to generate more cheer than frown, to offer more willingness than reluctance, and to enjoy being wholehearted. Amen.

55B Hymns
"For The Beauty Of The Earth" Tune: DIX
"God Made From One Blood" Tune: ST. DENIO
"O God, Whose Steadfast Love" or "Our Father, By Whose Name"
Tune: RHOSYMEDRE

Proper 20
Sunday between September 18 and September 24 inclusive

Second Lesson: James 3:13—4:3, 7-8a
Theme: Make Peace

Call To Worship

Leader: Who is wise and understanding among us?
People: Those who stay in touch with God.
Leader: Who is wise and understanding?
People: Those who seek to foster healing.
Leader: Let us strive to be wise and understanding.
People: Let us be makers of peace.

Collect

We are people searching for wisdom. Therefore, we draw near to you, O God, hoping that you will come closer to us and guide us toward leading better lives that will encourage peace in your world. Amen.

Prayer Of Confession

When self-interest threatens to promote general disorder in the world, we wonder how we can turn things around, O God, so that your wisdom will draw us to introduce a spirit of gentleness that encourages peace. Give us the patience to persevere in all peacemaking. Through the Holy Spirit. Amen.

55B Hymns

"Worship The Lord In The Beauty Of Holiness" Tune: MONSELL
"Touch The Earth Lightly" Tune: TENDERNESS
"O God Of Love, O God Of Peace" Tune: HESPERUS or "O God Of God, O Light Of Light" Tune: O GROSSER GOTT

Proper 20
Sunday between September 18 and September 24 inclusive

Gospel: Mark 9:30-37
Theme: One Little Child

Call To Worship
Leader: How do we welcome one little child in the name of Jesus?
People: With hope, with enthusiasm, with respect, with the open arms of our heart, with an attitude of love.
Leader: How do we welcome one little child in the name of Jesus?
People: By calling the child into responsibility, by finding time to listen, by conveying that we value the child, by teaching what is right, by feeding the child's whole being.

Collect
Compassionate God, we come as a church who wants to convey to children that this church home is a place that accepts thems, loves them, and welcomes them, one by one. Help us to bolster this hope by entrusting creative energy, our money, and the programs of the church for the nurture of children. Amen.

Prayer Of Confession
We like to think in terms of numbers, God, but numbers overlook that people count one by one. One by one is how you think of us. One by one is how you welcome us. One by one is how we reach out to you. Help us to welcome each child, one by one. In the name of Jesus the Christ. Amen.

55B Hymns
"Children Of God" or "O Brother Man, Fold To Thy Heart Thy Brother" Tune: WELWYN
"O Jesus, I Have Promised" or "O Savior, Precious Savior" Tune: ANGEL'S STORY
"Hope Of The World" Tune: VICAR

Proper 21
Sunday between September 25 and October 1 inclusive

First Lesson: Esther 7:1-6, 9-10; 9:20-22
Theme: Speaking Up

Call To Worship
Let us be filled with the courage of Queen Esther who, upon seeing an opportunity to make a difference, dared to speak up. Let us be filled with the selfless attitude of Esther in restoring freedom where freedom has been lost. Where injustice is epidemic, let us aim for what is just. Come, let us worship God who stands by us.

Collect
We come to you, O wise and just Creator, who has the capacity to turn us from sorrow into gladness and from mourning into rejoicing. Instill in us the confidence to approach those who can help the suffering gain relief from the enemies of abuse, poverty, and discrimination. Amen.

Prayer Of Confession
When we recognize a crossroad and have a chance to make a difference in the lives of those around us, show us, O God, the wisdom to focus on what is of highest importance and greatest value. We have good ideas and devise plans which we fail to accomplish. We are not lazy but lacking in bravery. Grant us the nerve to act on our hope. Amen.

56B Hymns[1]
"Creator Spirit, Come, We Pray" Tune: DICKINSON COLLEGE or PUER NOBIS NASCITUR
"God Our Author And Creator" Tune: JEFFERSON
"Where Cross The Crowded Ways Of Life" Tune: GERMANY

Proper 21
Sunday between September 25 and October 1 inclusive

Second Lesson: James 5:13-20
Theme: Prayer Advocate

Call To Worship
Prayer for one who suffers is an acceptable action. We are far from powerless in this process of healing. Prayer needs a request in order to begin. Prayer needs a pray-er to reconnect us with ourselves, with each other, and with God. Come, let us assume an attitude of prayer as we sing and speak and listen.

Collect
We come in faith to God, whose presence we summon at prayer in behalf of one who suffers. We come in trust to God, who hears us when we care enough to intercede. We come in wonder to God, whose ways of healing far surpass our understanding. Amen.

Prayer Of Confession
When we need an advocate in prayer, O God, let us not refrain from asking. Help us understand that by taking others into our confidence, we show not weakness but strength. Keep us ready for change so we might fully participate in the mystery of praying for each other. In the spirit of Jesus the Christ. Amen.

56B Hymns[1]
"It's Me, It's Me, O Lord," "Not My Brother, Nor My Sister," or
   "Standing In The Need Of Prayer" Tune: NEED OF PRAYER or
   PENITENT
"Our Father, Who From Heaven Above" Tune: VATER UNSER
"Nearer, My God, To [Thee][You]" Tune: BETHANY

Proper 21
Sunday between September 25 and October 1 inclusive

Gospel: Mark 9:38-50
Theme: Champion In His Name

Call To Worship
Be a champion for the ways of Christ. Be a wholehearted supporter of Christ. Put both your energy and your heart into holding Christ in first place in your life, above all else.

Collect
Just as Christ is for us, you are for us, O great Encourager, and we are for you. We come joyfully as cheerleaders because you steadily root for us. In the spirit of Christ. Amen.

Prayer Of Confession
Though we choose you as first in our lives, O God, we often fail to sustain our faith by actions that miscarry your teachings. Help us to avoid being our own stumbling blocks. Amen.

56B Hymns[1]
"I Love To Tell The Story" Tune: HANKEY
"We Offer Christ" Tune: CHARTERHOUSE
"We Love [Thy][Your] [Kingdom][Realm], O God" Tune: ST. THOMAS

---

1. Throughout the month, sing verse 4 of "Jesus Shall Reign" Tune: DUKE STREET as a closing response.

Proper 22
Sunday between October 2 and October 8 inclusive

First Lesson: Job 1:1, 2:1-10
Theme: Counting On God

Call To Worship
God appears to be supportive of us when things go right. In the midst of the easy times in life, we can count on God. God seems to let us down when things go wrong. In the midst of the messes of life, we also can count on God. Come, let us worship the Sustainer, the constant, steady presence in our lives.

Collect
Only by having the chance to practice turning away from wrong do we discover how strong we are because of you, O God. Only by having the chance to wrestle with evil's magnet do we discover how strong you are, O God. Hearten us throughout the journey so we might continue to choose you. Amen.

Prayer Of Confession
Sometimes, God, we wonder if being the best person we can be is worth it all. Then we realize that our focus has gone askew. You are the object of our trust and faithfulness. Because you made us and because we are connected to you, we can engage in hopeful living, surmount what we need to, and come out on the side of faith. Amen.

57B Hymns[1]
"All My Hope [On God] Is Firmly Grounded" Tune: MICHAEL or "My Hope Is Built On Nothing Less" Tune: MAGDALEN, MELITA, SOLID ROCK, or THE SOLID ROCK

"In The Very Midst Of Life" Tune: MITTEN WIR IM LEBEN SIND **OR** "In The Midst Of New Dimensions" Tune: NEW DIMENSIONS

"I Trust, O Christ, In You Alone" Tune: ALLEIN ZU DIR

Proper 22
Sunday between October 2 and October 8 inclusive

Second Lesson: Hebrews 1:1-4; 2:5-12
Theme: God's Mirror

Call To Worship
We are unable to observe ourselves directly, but only through the reflection of a mirror. Could it be that we see God reflectively through the fairness of others, our awareness of the creative process, in new ideas, acts of compassion, our own resolve to live decent lives? We do see God faithfully reflected through humanity.

Collect
God, you continually open up spiritual space within the room of the soul that wants to know you. You want to be known. You speak to us in many and various ways. Thank you for mirroring a true picture of yourself through Christ. Amen.

Prayer Of Confession
Dear God, help us to recognize you in the people around us. Help us to live in a way that others might draw closer to you. In the name of Christ. Amen.

57B Hymns[1]
"My Faith Looks Up To Thee" Tune: OLIVET
"I Know My Faith Is Founded" Tune: NUN LOB, MEIN SEEL
" 'Tis So Sweet To Trust In Jesus" Tune: TRUST IN JESUS

Proper 22
Sunday between October 2 and October 8 inclusive

Gospel: Mark 10:2-16
Theme: Finding Love

Call To Worship

Leader: When we find love, let us cherish it.

People: Some among us wonder if ever we will find a life mate.

Leader: Before we catch a glimpse of love, let us practice being lovable.

People: Some among us seem unable to sustain a loving relationship.

Leader: When we find love, let us grow and stretch it to reach beyond ourselves.

People: Some among us have lost a life mate to death.

Leader: When we have known love, let us remember its joy not measured by clock time.

All: When we find love, let us cherish it.

Collect

Your love, O God, is greater than our love, yet our choice to love is honorable. Because you first loved us, we also have the capacity to love others. Amen.

Prayer Of Confession

Dear God, loving is not always easy. Keep especially near to you those who associate love with its absence, with friction, or with disappointment. Keep especially near to you those who grieve a lost love. Keep especially near to you those who day by day are daring to season their love with ever-strengthening commitment. Amen.

57B Hymns[1]

"Jesus Loves Me" Tune: JESUS LOVES ME

"When Love Is Found" Tune: O WALY WALY

"I Am [Thine][Yours], O Lord" Tune: I AM [THINE][YOURS]

---

1. Throughout October, sing verse 3 of "Draw Us In The Spirit's Tether" Tune: UNION SEMINARY as a closing response.

Proper 23
Sunday between October 9 and October 15 inclusive

First Lesson: Job 23:1-9, 16-17
Theme: Where On Earth Are You?

Call To Worship

Leader: Where are you when we need you, God?

People: When our lives are ripped apart, all we can do is hope in you, God.

Leader: Where are you, God, when accident or disease or chance hurls all our plans, our future, our dreams into the wind?

People: When our lives are ripped apart, all we can do is hope in you, God.

Leader: Where are you, God, when we are in such turmoil that all we want to do is run away or worse?

People: When our lives are ripped apart, all we can do is hope in you, God.

All: Where on earth are you, God?

Collect

We trust in you, O Sustainer, to help us to move through the awful times toward healing. Amen.

Prayer Of Confession

When the burdens we carry overwhelm us, we speak nothing but complaint. When pain swallows us, we think of nothing else. Help us to hold on, God. Stay by us. Support us with your healing when we are afraid, when we feel hopeless, when we are weary of it all. Amen.

58B Hymns

"O God, My God" Tune: O GOD, MY GOD
"When The Winds Rage All Around Us" Tune: WE TRUST IN YOU
"I Walk In Danger All The Way" Tune: DER LIEBEN SONNE LICHT UND PRACHT

Proper 23
Sunday between October 9 and October 15 inclusive

Second Lesson: Hebrews 4:12-16
Theme: You Know, Don't You, Jesus?

Call To Worship
You know how it is with us, don't you, Jesus? When prejudice enslaves. When murder seems to be the norm. When relationships strain to breaking. When burdens deplete our reserves. When hope vanishes. You know how it is.

Collect
Because you know how it is with us, O compassionate Healer, we freely give you the thoughts and intentions of our heart. Because we need not hide our weaknesses from you, we can stand before you with open souls. We come not in fear but with trust. In the name of Christ. Amen.

Prayer Of Confession
We get it all turned around, God. We think we are in this all alone, then see that you do not observe from a safe distance. You put your own life in jeopardy by coming in human form. You know how it is with us, don't you, Jesus? Amen.

58B Hymns
"Oh, Love, How Deep" Tune: DEO GRACIAS
"Healing River Of The Spirit" Tune: BEACH SPRING or JOEL
"What A Friend We Have In Jesus" Tune: CONVERSE or ERIE

Proper 23
Sunday between October 9 and October 15 inclusive

Gospel: Mark 10:17-31
Theme: Are You Sure?

Call To Worship
Are you sure, Jesus, that with God all things are possible? That we are not just wistful? The ideals you offer are high. You call us to stretch to our finest. No one can be that good all the time.

Collect
We look to you, O faithful One, to be our guide as we move through the daily muck of chagrin, conflict, and letting ourselves down. Despite our inconsistencies, move us toward the possible. In the name of Jesus the Christ. Amen.

Prayer Of Confession
Strengthen us when we become disheartened, O God. Stand by us, you who calls us to accept the challenge of being Christian. In case you are right that we can raise the level of human relationships, let us practice justice, doing what is right, and being truthful. For the sake of Jesus Christ. Amen.

58B Hymns
"Jesus, Your Boundless Love So True" Tune: VATER UNSER
"I Look To [Thee][You] In Every Need" Tune: O JESU
"Faithful God, You Have Been Our Guide" Tune: LINSTEAD

Proper 24
Sunday between October 16 and October 22 inclusive

First Lesson: Job 38:1-7 (34-41)
Theme: You Upstart!

Call To Worship
By whatever name we call God, God is there. God is listening and speaking into our silences. God is waiting and ready during our shouting. God is present as we sigh.

Collect
Holy God, we praise your name. Holy God, we call to you. Holy God, we wait for you. Amen.

Prayer Of Confession
Sometimes, God, happenings jolt us out of any assumption that we are in control of our life. They shake out of us any last piece of confidence, any final chip of arrogance. Having no one higher to blame in our earthquake, we end up shouting to you, "What are you doing, God?" Then, startled, we begin to listen to your questions. Forgive our conceit. Amen.

59B Hymns
"Holy God, We Praise [Thy][Your] Name" Tune: GROSSER GOTT, WIR LOBEN DICH
"By Whatever Name We Call You" Tune: OGONTZ
"God, Whose Giving Knows No Ending" Tune: AUSTRIAN HYMN

Proper 24
Sunday between October 16 and October 22 inclusive

Second Lesson: Hebrews 5:1-10
Theme: Called Forever

Call To Worship
God calls us to take seriously our jobs, work, and professions even in times of low job security. When we greet our work with an attitude that anticipates high quality and satisfaction of purpose, an integrity surrounds us that has little to do with length of time or amount of money.

Collect
You offer to your people, O God, the sustenance of having a purpose and a sense of meaning. You bring us energy of spirit for accomplishing our daily tasks despite weaknesses and frailties. We give you thanks for your bolstering support. Amen.

Prayer Of Confession
We are told, God, that we are better people for our suffering. Suffering makes us stronger. Suffering hones us to use our energy only on what is of greatest importance. We are not certain that we believe these words, God. Teach us how to persevere and to trust in the nearness of your Spirit in carrying out the work to which you call us. Amen.

59B Hymns
"Holy, Holy, Holy" Tune: NICAEA
"Trust And Obey" Tune: TRUST AND OBEY
"O For A Heart To Praise My God" Tune: RICHMOND

Proper 24
Sunday between October 16 and October 22 inclusive

Gospel: Mark 10:35-45
Theme: We Are Able, But

Call To Worship

Leader: Are you able to live out the promises of being a Christian? We say that we are able.

People: The question is, will we choose to live as Christians amid the school sports events, television and internet, the job competition, the list of pressing other things?

Leader: Are you able to live out the promises of being a Christian? We say that we are able.

People: We are able, but —.

Collect

You, O Strength, who offers guidance for our hands, our feet, our thoughts, our heart, guide our intentions toward being the best people we can be according to what you teach us through Christ. Amen.

Prayer Of Confession

Do you know, God, that just because we seem too busy to take time to live as Christians, that does not mean we no longer respect the teachings of our faith? Help us to reconcile our hearts so we do not give up on ourselves altogether and stop trying to practice our faith. We hear your voice calling as we harvest our talents. Help us want to turn a listening ear to you. For the sake of Christ. Amen.

59B Hymns

"[Ye][You] Servants Of God" Tune: HANOVER
"Guide My Feet" Tune: GUIDE MY FEET
"Jesus Calls Us, O'er The Tumult" Tune: GALILEE or "Hark, The Voice Of Jesus Calling" Tune: GALILEAN

Proper 25
Sunday between October 23 and October 29 inclusive

First Lesson: Job 42:1-6, 10-17
Theme: Seeing For Ourselves

Call To Worship
Like a parent who must insist because a child's life direction is in
jeopardy, God persists with us until we can see for ourselves the right
path. Then all is left behind for rejoicing and new life.

Collect
We rejoice in the freedom of your forgiveness, O God. We rejoice
in the tenderness of your gathering us into what is right. We celebrate
the new life you make possible. Amen.

Prayer Of Confession
When we are at the height of turmoil, fearing that we will founder
if we give in at all, something quiet lets go inside us. Okay, God, I
have had enough, we admit. We allow you to take over. Though we
cannot stand ourselves, something releases even this attitude. We
change. Through you, we are in charge of our lives again. Thank
you, God. Amen.

60B Hymns
"I Need [Thee][You] Every Hour" Tune: NEED or "When In The
    Hour Of Deepest Need" Tune: WENN WIR IN HÖCHSTEIN
    NÖTEN SEIN
"There's A Wideness In God's Mercy" Tune: IN BABILONE
"Hear The Voice Of God, So Tender" Tune: BEACH SPRING or
    RAQUEL

Proper 25
Sunday between October 23 and October 29 inclusive

Second Lesson: Hebrews 7:23-28
Theme: Once And For All

Call To Worship
The truths about Christ are as true for people today as they were for the people of his day. Once and for all, Christ offered himself for us. Once and for all, Christ has promised our redemption. Come, let us worship God in the enduring truth of these words. Let us stand on the empowering presence of his promises.

Collect
Unlike changes in teachers, caregivers, and employers, your constancy offers us a lasting relationship. You know us well. We need not begin from the beginning each time we talk to you. Your promises are firm. Through Christ. Amen.

Prayer Of Confession
There is something deeply settling, O God, about the once and for all of the acts of Jesus Christ. We yearn for permanence because so much change enters our lives. You have provided firm stability in the life, death, and resurrection of Christ. We are grateful for the peace you bring. Through our Savior. Amen.

60B Hymns
"How Deep The Silence Of The Soul" Tune: TALLIS' THIRD TUNE
"O God In Heaven" Tune: HALAD
"Standing On The Promises" Tune: PROMISES

Proper 25
Sunday between October 23 and October 29 inclusive

Gospel: Mark 10:46-52
Theme: No-Fault Healing

Call To Worship
Leader: God blesses us in times of darkness as well as light.
People: God blesses us in times of weakness as well as strength.
All: Come, let us receive the love of the tolerant Creator who recognizes our faith and blesses us with a healing Spirit.

Collect
As we travel together walking side by side with our neighbors, show us the wisdom to reduce our penchant to judge. Guide us so that our works avoid becoming good-doing that ignores the dignity of those we try to help. In the name of Jesus the Christ. Amen.

Prayer Of Confession
Healer God, remind us to uncurl our own spirits so we can be open to see the needs of our neighbors and will choose to embrace their distresses with our faith and acts of kindness. For the sake of Christ. Amen.

60B Hymns
"Amazing Grace" Tune: AMAZING GRACE
"I Heard The Voice Of Jesus Say" Tune: THIRD MODE MELODY
"God Of Our Life" Tune: SANDON

Proper 26
Sunday between October 30 and November 5 inclusive

First Lesson: Ruth 1:1-18
Theme: Secure

Call To Worship
Leader: Like Ruth's faithfulness to Naomi, our Sustainer is determined to offer strength to God's people.
People: God is security in our insecure times.
Leader: Where you go, I will go.
People: God is security in our insecure times.
Leader: Where you lodge, I will lodge.
People: God is security in insecure times. Thank God.

Collect
We gather before you, O God of hope, trusting you to guide us through all the chapters of our life. Teach us that we need not always understand your mysterious ways. You bring us fresh courage as we see your hand in unfolding plans. Amen.

Prayer Of Confession
As we become certain that the one stable element in our lives is change, you, O God, remind us that we can gain security in our determination to stand by our choice to treat others right and to live by truth. We see then that no change can shake us loose from the firm rock of your guidance. In the name of the Holy Spirit. Amen.

61B Hymns[1]
"God Moves In A Mysterious Way" Tune: DUNDEE
"I Will Trust In The Lord" Tune: TRUST IN THE LORD
"If [You][Thou] But Trust In God To Guide [Thee][You]" Tune: NEUMARK

Proper 26
Sunday between October 30 and November 5 inclusive

Second Lesson: Hebrews 9:11-14
Theme: From Dead Works

Call To Worship
Leader: Dead works keep us on a dead-end road of non-living.
People: We are people who follow the Spirit of the living God.
Leader: Dead works are without aim, meaning, or vitality.
People: We are people, curious about the Spirit of the living God.
Leader: Dead works have nothing to do with the living Spirit within us.
People: We worship the living Spirit of God.

Collect
Dear God, your Spirit infuses our lives with an energy that transforms imprudence into wisdom and changes doubt to courage for greeting life. Your Spirit keeps us on the course of integrity. Your Spirit keeps us in touch with the core of our being. Amen.

Prayer Of Confession
We know about dead works, God. They waste our time, sap our energy, exhaust our soul, and keep us circling without growth. Fill our lives with the strength of your vitality so we might know fullness of life. Through Christ. Amen.

61B Hymns[1]
"God Of Grace And God Of Glory" Tune: CWM RHONDDA
"We Are [God's][Your] People" Tune: WHITFIELD
"Spirit Of The Living God" Tune: IVERSON[2]

---

1. Throughout November, sing one of the first three verses of "Won't You Let Me Be Your Servant?" Tune: SERVANT SONG as a prayer response or a closing response.

2. The one-verse hymn lends itself well to singing without accompaniment. Dividing the congregation into two sections, try it as a two-part round with Part B beginning when Part A starts the third line. Sing twice. It also works as a three-part round with each successive part beginning as the second and then the third lines are sung. Sing three times.

Proper 26
Sunday between October 30 and November 5 inclusive

Gospel: Mark 12:28-34
Theme: With All Your Heart

Call To Worship
Leader: Love God with all your heart;
People: Not with lip service words but with wholehearted energy.
Leader: Love God with all your soul;
People: Not with a little corner of your soul but with your whole being.
Leader: Love God with all your mind;
People: Not with emotion only but with your fullest capacity for understanding.
Leader: Love God with all your strength;
People: Not with what is left over at the end of the day, but with rested, morning vigor ready to sprint into action.

Collect
When we put you first in our lives, O God, the rest of our living improves. We see you wherever we go, in whatever we do, and in whomever we meet. We approach all our days with new enthusiasm, deeper compassion, and renewed commitment. All praise to you, O God. Amen.

Prayer Of Confession
We bring you our broken hearts, O God. We offer our uneasy souls. We come with fragments of understanding. We approach you with faulty strength. We turn to you when our all seems small and inept, and you still honor us with all your love. Amen.

61B Hymns[1]
"Glorious Things Of [Thee][You] Are Spoken" Tune: AUSTRIA
"Community Of Christ" Tune: LEONI
"Renew Your Church" Tune: ALL IS WELL

Proper 27
Sunday between November 6 and November 12 inclusive

First Lesson: Ruth 3:1-5, 4:13-17
Theme: Strategy

Call To Worship
Ruth's loyalty to Naomi was rewarded by Naomi's wise guidance for doing what was practical for survival in their day. Like the women of the neighborhood who named Ruth's baby, let us bring to others the supportive nurture of nearby women. Let us build a sense of encouraging community within the neighborhood that is this church.

Collect
Gracious God, we bring to you hearts willing to help. Bring to us the insight that can strengthen in those we know the commitments holding their daily lives together. Amen.

Prayer Of Confession
Help us to plot and plan and strategize for the right reasons, God. When we find ourselves in a strange neighborhood, keep us brave, increase our wisdom, and draw us to the people in whom we can put our trust. Help us reach out to each other as a faithful and faith-filled church family. Amen.

62B Hymns
"Joyful, Joyful, We Adore [Thee][You]" Tune: HYMN TO JOY
"Be Not Dismayed" or "God Will Take Care Of You" Tune: MARTIN
"For The Faithful Who Have Answered" Tune: OMNI DIE

Proper 27
Sunday between November 6 and November 12 inclusive

Second Lesson: Hebrews 9:24-28
Theme: Finally

Call To Worship
Christ died once and for all on our behalf and yet, like a gentle, enduring Spirit, Christ faithfully continues to enter our waiting lives again and again bringing quiet, life-giving hope.

Collect
Into the sin of laziness, into the sin of mental or physical cruelty, into the sin of guilty living, and into all the other sin that separates us from God, our neighbors, and ourselves, you come, O Christ, offering your transforming hope to those who wait for you. Hear the invitation of our prayer. Through Christ. Amen.

Prayer Of Confession
We recognize, O God, that, unlike Christ, no progress is final for us. We appear to move forward in our lives, then we backslide. Help us to garner strength for the living of each day within the freedom Christ's sacrifice has given us to surmount what seems insurmountable. Amen.

62B Hymns
"Immortal, Invisible, God Only Wise" Tune: ST. DENIO
"Great Is [Thy][Your] Faithfulness" Tune: FAITHFULNESS
"How Like A Gentle Spirit" Tune: SURSUM CORDA

Proper 27
Sunday between November 6 and November 12 inclusive

Gospel: Mark 12:38-44
Theme: All

Call To Worship
Wherein lies your poverty? There is the source of our compassion. There we identify with others who also suffer. There we most want to help. There we give of our energy, wisdom, experience, and understanding so that another might improve, so that another might know we join the journey into hope.

Collect
When we give of ourselves in service, our attention is on others rather than on ourselves. Instead of sensing depletion of our energy, we know fullness of spirit and purpose. Giving of ourselves, like loving, opens us more fully to you, O God. In the name of Christ. Amen.

Prayer Of Confession
Dear God, help us to rise above our selfishness, our greed, and our desire to be noticed and praised. Move us, rather, toward the compassionate giving of ourselves. In the name of Christ. Amen.

62B Hymns
"Christian, Rise And Act [Thy][Your] Creed" Tune: INNOCENTS
"I Would Be True" Tune: PEEK
"Teach Me, [O][Lord][My God], [Thy Way][Your Holy Way]" Tune:
    MORNINGTON or ROCKINGHAM

Proper 28
Sunday between November 13 and November 19 inclusive

First Lesson: 1 Samuel 1:4-20
Theme: A Sad Heart

Call To Worship

A sad heart needs to pray, to speak honestly to God, to sort out and clarify what is the trouble. A sad heart requires attending to, understanding, kindness, and time.

Collect

When we are sad-hearted, we need to receive compassion so we can recognize the love that is all around us. When we find others who carry a sad heart, help us to meet them with the right questions, O God, so they might begin to talk and we might begin to listen in a helpful way. Amen.

Prayer Of Confession

When we become troubled, O God, help us remember first to turn to you. Teach us to pray with sighs and silence until we find the words to tell you what we need to say. Teach us to pray, God, trusting that you are listening with the same intensity as we are praying. Through the Spirit of Christ. Amen.

63B Hymns

"Prayer Is The Soul's Sincere Desire" Tune: CAMPMEETING

"Sweet Hour Of Prayer" Tune: SWEET HOUR

"I Leave All Things To God's Direction" Tune: WER NUR DEN LIEBEN GOTT

Proper 28
Sunday between November 13 and November 19 inclusive

Second Lesson: Hebrew 10:11-14 (15-18) 19-25
Theme: Encouraging One Another

Call To Worship
Leader: Let us approach one another with a true heart in full assurance of faith.
People: **We want to generate love rather than discord and engender worthy achievement rather than failure.**
Leader: Let us approach our work with a true heart in full assurance of faith.
People: **We hope to kindle among our co-workers a spirit of healthy community.**
All: **Now let us approach God with a true heart in full assurance of faith.**

Collect
Because we can accomplish little alone, O God, we gather in this place in the name of Christ to offer one another encouragement in our faith. Be with us, guide our ways, and hearten our spirit. Through Christ. Amen.

Prayer Of Confession
We know, O God, that all our living — our caring, our helping, our giving — reflects the faith we have in you. Rejoice with us when our faith flowers. Strengthen us when it falters. Remind us always of our freedom through Christ to try again the new and living way. Amen.

63B Hymns
"Draw Us In The Spirit's Tether" Tune: UNION SEMINARY
"Savio[u]r, Like A Shepherd Lead Us" Tune: BRADBURY
"Where Charity And Love Prevail" Tune: ST. PETER

Proper 28
Sunday between November 13 and November 19 inclusive

Gospel: Mark 13:1-8
Theme: Birthpangs Of Change

Call To Worship

Leader: Into the birthing of change —
People: The birthing of an idea, a new business,
Leader: A new lifestyle, a new honesty, a new way of meeting life,
People: An infant —
Leader: Into all of this change comes at once the sharpening of our sense of threat and the vigor of expectation.

Collect

As the birthpangs of change intensify in the midst of a broken world, Creator God, sustain our wisdom and fortify our hope of wholeness. As new realities push toward birth, increase our curiosity and our appreciation of life's wanting to be in full, healthy creation. Amen.

Prayer Of Confession

Be with us, Giver of hope, in the letting go time before we allow change to happen. Then we are hesitant, then we are afraid, then we are taut springs. Remind us that we are builders because of our faith and because of the evidence of your faith in us. Through Christ. Amen.

63B Hymns

"We Would Be Building" Tune: FINLANDIA
"Behold A Broken World" Tune: MARSH CHAPEL
"Christ Will Come Again" Tune: IDA

Proper 29 (Christ The King)
Sunday between November 20 and November 26 inclusive

First Lesson: 2 Samuel 23:1-7
Theme: Touchable

Call To Worship
Leader: When we are without God, we are untouchable thorns.
People protect themselves from us and keep their distance.
**People: When we are with God, we become touchable and kind.
People sense an invitation and approach us.**

Collect
Gracious God, we yearn to be in a right relationship with you,
with ourselves, and with those around us. In a rebirth of connecting,
let the deserts of our relationships burst into soft flower and dance in
the wind. Amen.

Prayer Of Confession
Dear God, when we become so overwhelmed by our loads of work,
life, and family that we present our thorny side, draw us nearer to you.
Quiet our weariness so we might heed the strength of your transforming presence. Amen.

64B Hymns
"Morning Has Broken" Tune: BUNESSAN
"Strengthen All The Weary Hands" Tune: SONG OF REJOICING
"O Day Of God, Draw Near" Tune: ST. MICHAEL

Proper 29 (Christ The King)
Sunday between November 20 and November 26 inclusive

Second Lesson: Revelation 1:4b-8
Theme: To God Who Loves Us

Call To Worship

Leader: A salute to almighty God who loves us and frees us and created us to be part of God's realm:

All: **To God who is, who was, who is to come:**
To you, the Alpha and the Omega:
To you, Creator, Savior, and Sustainer:
To you, we give glory and power forever. Amen.

Collect

Today — this year, this century — is within your realm of alpha and omega, O God. You have become neither outmoded nor irrelevant. You are still at all our beginnings. You are still at our endings. You are still everywhere in between. All praise to you, O faithful, mighty one. Amen.

Prayer Of Confession

No matter how often we try to push you aside, O God, or how busily we attempt to forget about you, you still are and will be. You find a way to come to us. Forgive our making you trivial in our lives. Accept our gratitude for your persistent coming. Through Christ. Amen.

64B Hymns

"Jesus Shall Reign" Tune: DUKE STREET

"Lo, He Comes With Clouds Descending" Tune: HELMSLEY or PICARDY

"All Hail The Power Of Jesus' Name" Tune: CORONATION

196

Proper 29 (Christ The King)
Sunday between November 20 and November 26 inclusive

Gospel: John 18:33-37
Theme: Mystery, Mystery

Call To Worship
We proclaim God as sovereign. We belong to the truth. We listen to God's voice. Come, let us worship God who reigns with the mysterious power of love and hope and truth.

Collect
We hear your voice in the truths our highest laws point to, O victorious, reigning God. We hear your voice in the fair acts that reflect relationships governed by love. We hear your voice in the hope welling up within us with sufficient vigor to keep us going. All praise to you, O living God. Amen.

Prayer Of Confession
We proclaim you sovereign, O God, within a world that appears oblivious to authority. Perhaps, God, you are that power enabling us to persist in talking out troubling issues. Perhaps you are the one who empowers us to persevere in the struggle for what is just and right. Perhaps you are the creative force behind imagination, the birth of ideas, and discovery. Even as we ponder, the mystery of your being draws us to your truth. In the Spirit of Christ. Amen.

64B Hymns
"[Ye][You] Servants Of God, Your [Master][Sovereign] Proclaim" or
    "O Worship The King" Tune: HANOVER
"Enter In The Realm Of God" Tune: DANDANSOY
"Rejoice, Give Thanks And Sing" or "Rejoice, The Lord Is King"
    Tune: DARWALL'S 148TH

Reformation Sunday

First Lesson: Jeremiah 31:31-34
Theme: I Will Be Your God

Call To Worship
When we realize that God comes to us within the kindness of forgiving love, we release our fear of God. God is no longer a distant theory but one close enough for us to trust enough to disclose our failings. Come and worship in the knowledge that God is our God and that all are God's people.

Collect
Your covenant with us is strong, O God, so that nothing can cause it to break. Your covenant is inclusive so that no one is left out. Your promise speaks to our hearts so that we cannot miss your intent. All praise to you, O God. Amen.

Prayer Of Confession
When a law is external to us, we have ways of excluding ourselves from its authority. We know that we are not above your law, O God. Your rules have no loopholes. They reach into everyone's heart and change forever the way we treat others. Amen.

65B Hymns
"A Mighty Fortress Is Our God" Tune: EIN' FESTE BURG
"Now Bless The God Of Israel" Tune: FOREST GREEN
"Oh, How Great Is Your Compassion" Tune: ACH, WAS SOLL ICH
    SÜNDER MACHEN

Reformation Sunday

Second Lesson: Romans 3:19-28
Theme: Cleared

Call To Worship
Because faith in God clears us from the sinful part of our life, it also clears us for the grateful response that leads to carrying out worthwhile achievements. Come, let us give thanks to God.

Collect
O God, who cheers us on our way and who inspires us to live beyond ourselves, to you we give hearty thanks. We, who fall short, can know a new beginning because of our faith in you and your faith in us, O forgiving Creator. Amen.

Prayer Of Confession
O God, help us to do the works that make a difference in our world for the right reason. Let the grace you gave us by the sacrifice of Christ permeate our being through and through. Let us be aware that you are our greatest champion and defender. Through Christ. Amen.

65B Hymns
"Salvation Unto Us Has Come" Tune: ES IST DAS HEIL
"God's Word Is Our Great Heritage" Tune: REUTER
"Now Thank We All Our God" Tune: NUN DANKET

Reformation Sunday

Gospel: John 8:31-36
Theme: Freed

Call To Worship

Leader: We know freedom in Christ:
People: We are freed to move on from disappointment;
Leader: Freed to leave behind finished and unfinished chapters;
People: Freed to abandon destructive ways of being;
Leader: Freed from guilt;
All: Freed to make new beginnings.

Collect

We gather as followers of Christ, who want to know the truth. Your truth, O generous Sustainer, will make us free from all that separates us from you, from our neighbor, and from ourselves. We pray in the name of him who is the way, the truth, and the life. Amen.

Prayer Of Confession

Unless we live in truth, we cannot live as people of authenticity. Unless we live with integrity, we cannot know a sense of inner peace. Help us, O God, to take advantage of the strength of truth. Amen.

65B Hymns

"This Is A Day Of New Beginnings" Tune: BEGINNINGS
"By Grace I'm Saved" Tune: O DASS ICH TAUSEND ZUNGEN HÄTTE
"I Know My Faith Is Founded" Tune: NUN LOB, MEIN SEEL

All Saints' Sunday

First Lesson: Isaiah 25:6-9
Theme: Wiping Away The Tears

Call To Worship

Come and worship God, who is all-powerful and so gentle as to wipe away the tears from our faces. Come and worship God, who takes fear out of death. Come and worship God, who absorbs all death into the whole company of God's being.

Collect

You, O God, were the rock, the refuge, and the strength for the saints who endured and went before us. You, O God, bring stability, security, and courage to our enduring and to our going out. To these truths, we sing alleluia. Amen.

Prayer Of Confession

All of our lives, we have been longing for you, O God. Though we still are filled with pondering and wondering, we anticipate a grand reunion with all who have gone before us. We cannot know the details now, but we live our lives within the trust of your redemptive gathering in. Through Christ. Amen.

66B Hymns

"For All The Saints" Tune: SINE NOMINE
"Give Thanks For Life" Tune: ROBINSON
"The Church's One Foundation" Tune: AURELIA

All Saints' Sunday

Second Lesson: Revelation 21:1-6a
Theme: God, Alpha And Omega

Call To Worship

On this All Saints' Sunday, we remember the faithful people in the history of the church. We wonder in what manner they are living beyond the earthly form. We cannot know this now any more than we can know what this new "place" will be like. What we can do is trust that God, who is the beginning and the end, will be present. Come, let us worship God, the Alpha and the Omega.

Collect

O God, who is present at our physical birth and death and who is at all other transitions in our life, we praise you for offering us new beginnings. You make all things as new as the start of a day. We trust you now and at our ending. In the name of Christ. Amen.

Prayer Of Confession

We wonder, O God, about what we cannot yet perceive. We know that our imaginings of life after death reflect our individual yearnings. If the physical body suffers now, later all suffering will cease. If our relating to others has been troublesome, later all such distress will be in the past. Bear with us, O God, until the time comes and we will know and finally will relax into your care. Amen.

66B Hymns

"Come, Let Us Join With Faithful Souls" or "The Savior Calls; Let Every Ear" Tune: AZMON

"O What Their Joy And Their Glory Must Be" Tune: O QUANTA QUALIA

"O Savior, For The Saints" Tune: FESTAL SONG

All Saints' Sunday

Gospel: John 11:32-44
Theme: Beginning To Weep

Call To Worship
When Jesus saw the grief of Mary after the death of her brother
Lazarus, he began to weep. The shortest verse in the Bible, "Jesus
wept," brings us close to Jesus. We sense that God understands and
accepts our tears when we begin to weep.

Collect
Help us, O God, to endure the regrets, the blame and self-blame,
the anger, and all the other emotions of loss when we have sorrow.
Guide us through the craziness that overtakes our lives. Through the
presence of Christ. Amen.

Prayer Of Confession
Amid our tears of grief, we fear losing control, O God. Can we
survive another hour or the rest of our lives? Faith travels far from
our house door. We even wonder where you are, God, as the "why's"
rush in. Yet, because you, too, have wept, you know about the hole
within our heart. Amen.

66B Hymns
"Sorrow And Grief Had Come" Tune: OLIVET
"Since You Have, Too, Encountered Grief" Tune: DUNDEE
"Lord Of Sorrows, Lord Of Grief" Tune: HEINLEIN

Day Of Thanksgiving

First Lesson: Joel 2:21-27
Theme: At The Root

Call To Worship
Take up the song of thanksgiving to God that the world has sung since the beginning of time. Carry the song of thanksgiving forward into the new century and new millennium. Sing your thanksgiving song until all people everywhere tap their feet to the song of hope. Come, O thankful people, come.

Collect
We come this day of giving thanks to share what we have with others. We offer a generous spirit. We bring an attitude of peace. We put into action our stewardship of the earth. We extend the hand of friendship to those of diverse circumstances. We rededicate ourselves to you, O God, by showing our thanks in how we live. Amen.

Prayer Of Confession
We confess, O generous Creator, that we take for granted the great things you have done. We pause on this day of thanksgiving to voice our gratitude. Be a constant reminder, O God, of the ways a thankful heart can influence the entire realm of human relationship. Amen.

67B Hymns
"Come, [O][Ye] Thankful People, Come" Tune: ST. GEORGE'S WINDSOR
"How Great Thou Art" Tune: HOW GREAT
"Take Up The Song" Tune: ELLERS

Day Of Thanksgiving

Second Lesson: 1 Timothy 2:1-7
Theme: Thanksgivings For Everyone

Call To Worship

Leader: Give prayers of thanksgiving for everyone.
People: There is one Architect for all God's creation.
Leader: Give prayers of request for everyone.
People: There is one Savior for all God's creation.
Leader: Give intercessory prayers for everyone.
All: There is one Listener for all God's creation.

Collect

We sing songs of thanksgiving with voices united, O God, and find the renewal of one Spirit. Hear our songs of thanksgiving, O God, and know our rejoicing that you are God of all. Amen.

Prayer Of Confession

When we start giving thanks for everything, Gracious God, something happens within us. We reach farther beyond ourselves than ordinary. We reach more deeply into ourselves than usual. We see others in a different light. We are surprised by an ever-extending sense of gratitude. Remind us, O God, to live with a daily attitude of thanksgiving. In the name of Christ. Amen.

67B Hymns

"We Praise [Thee][You] O God" Tune: KREMSER
"In Everything Give Thanks" Tune: ST. MICHAEL
"We Give [Thee][You] But [Thine][Your] Own" Tune: ENERGY or
    YATTENDON 46

Day Of Thanksgiving

Gospel: Matthew 6:25-33
Theme: Unnerved?

Call To Worship

Leader: Do not worry about your life.

People: Will we have enough food and drink to sustain us?

Leader: Do not worry about your life, God will see that you have enough to eat.

People: Will we have enough clothing and shoes and coats?

Leader: God knows all your needs and will attend to them. Put your energy into living the right kind of life.

All: We give thanks to you, O gracious and giving Sustainer. Amen.

Collect

You have reminded us, O God, that life is more than food and the body is more than clothing. You show us again and again that we are of great value to you and that we can have great courage in the certainty of your preparation for our well-being. Amen.

Prayer Of Confession

When we become unnerved, even in the midst of thanksgiving, help us, O God, to remember your kindness toward us and your generous spirit. Let us pause today from fretting to consider your gifts to us. In this plenty, take our gifts, God, and let us love you with hearts filled with thanksgiving. Amen.

67B Hymns

"Praise And Thanksgiving" or "Living With Birthing" Tune: BUNESSAN

"[Be Not Dismayed][God Will Take Care Of You]" Tune: MARTIN

"Take My Gifts" Tune: TALAVERA TERRACE

Index Of Hymns

AUS TIEFER N	From Depths Of Woe	MSL	49B
"	Out Of The Depths I	LCA, UMH	20B, 49B
AUSTIN	Like A Mother Who H	NCH	10B
AUSTRIA[N]	Glorious Things Of	LCA, MSL, NCH, PH, PRH, UMH	34B, 61B
"	God, Whose Giving Kn	NCH	59B
AUTHORITY	Silence! Frenzied,	NCH, UMH	12B
AVE VIRGO	Come, Ye Faithful,	LCA, PH, UMH	28B
AVON	As Pants The Hart	LCA, NCH	43B
"	As The Hart Longs	PRH	43B
AWAY IN A	Away In a Manger	LCA, MSL, NCH, PH, PRH, UMH	05B
AZMON	Come, Let Us Join	NCH, PH	35B, 47B, 66B
"	[O][Oh] For A Thous	NCH, UMH	13B
"	O For A World	NCH	16B, 27B
"	The Savior Calls; L	MSL	35B, 47B, 66B
"	You Gave My Heart	COC	30B, 44B

B

BALM	There Is A Balm In	NCH, PRH, UMH	43B
BANGOR	According To Thy	LCA, PH, PRH	26B
BATTLE HYMN	[My] Mine Eyes Hav	LCA, NCH, PH, PRH, UMH	24B
BEACH SPRIN	Hear The Voice Of	NCH	60B
"	Healing River Of	COC	58B
BEACON HILL	Are Ye Able	UMH	16B
BEATITUDO	[O][Oh] For A Thous	MSL	13B
BEECHER	Called As Partners	NCH	29B
"	Love Divine, All Lov	LCA, MSL, NCH, PH, PRH, UMH	07B, 31B
BEGINNINGS	This Is A Day Of New	NCH, UMH	37B, 65B
BENJAMIN	Spirit Of Jesus, If	NCH	53B
BETHANY	Nearer, My God, To	LCA, MSL, NCH, PH, UMH	56B
BISHOPGAR	Who Trusts In God A	MSL, PH	46B
BLAIRGOWRIE	O Young And Fearles	UMH	14B
BLANTYRE	That Boy-Child Of Ma	UMH	07B
BLOTT EN DA	Day By Day	PRH	40B
BOUNDLES	Come, O Spirit, Wit	NCH, PRH	36B
BOURBON	It Was A Sad And S	NCH	26B
BOYLSTON	A Charge To Keep I	PRH, UMH	13B, 40B
"	We Thank You God	COC	48B
BRADBURY	Savio[u]r, Like A Sh	LCA, NCH, PH, PRH, UMH	29B, 63B
BRED DINA V	O Word Made Flesh A	COC	04B, 07B
BRIDEGROOM	From The Crush Of	NCH	49B
"	Like The Murmur Of	NCH, UMH	33B
BRING A TOR	Bring A Torch, Jeann	PH	05B
BUNESSAN	Living With Birthing	GG	67B
"	Morning Has Broken	PH, PRH, UMH	08B, 52B, 64B
"	O The Deep, Deep Lo	PRH	25B
"	Praise And Thanksgi	MSL, UMH	52B, 67B

BY AND BY	We Are Often Tosse	NCH	42B
"	We'll Understand I	PRH, UMH	42B

C

CAMPMEETING	Prayer Is The Soul'	LCA, NCH, UMH	63B
CANONBURY	[God][Lord], Speak	LCA, NCH, PH, PRH, UMH	54B
"	Pray For A World	COC	53B
CANTERBURY	Holy Spirit, [Truth	LCA, NCH, PH, UMH	51B
CHARTERHOUSE	God, Bless Our Hom	NCH	13B
"	We Offer Christ	NCH	56B
CHEREPONI	Jesu, Jesu, Fill U	NCH, UMH	26B
CHILDREN	Pray For A World	COC	53B
CHRIST AROS	Up From The Grave	UMH	28B
CHRISTE SANC	Father, We Praise T	LCA, MSL, NCH, PH, UMH	29B
"	Rising In The Darkn	NCH	29B
CHRISTIAN LO	Where Charity And Lo	NCH, UMH	26B, 31B
CHRISTMAS	Awake, My Soul, Str	LCA, NCH, PH	14B, 43B
CTMAS SONG	There's A Song In	UMH	01B
CHRISTOPHER	What Wondrous Love	NCH, UMH	27B
CONDITOR AL	Creator Of The Star	NCH, PH, UMH	01B
"	O Lord Of Light, Wh	MSL	01B
"	O Loving Founder Of	NCH	01B
CONSOLATIO	My Shepherd Is The	NCH	31B
CONSTANTINE	God Of Abraham And	NCH	21B
CONVERSE	What A Friend We	MSL	19B, 58B
CORONATION	All Hail The Power	MSL, NCH, PH, PRH, UMH	64B
CRANHAM	In The Bleak Midwin	LCA, NCH, PH, UMH	02B, 08B
CRUCIFIER	Lift High The Cross	MSL, NCH, PRH, UMH	22B
CWM RHONDDA	For The Healing	NCH, UMH	12B, 34B, 49B
"	God Of Grace And Go	MSL, NCH, PH, PRH UMH	01B, 32B, 61B
"	Guide Me, O My [Tho	LCA, MSL, NCH, PH, PRH	21B, 49B

D

DANDANSOY	Enter In The Realm	NCH	64B
DARWALL'S 1	Rejoice, Give Thank	NCH	64B
"	Rejoice, The Lord I	MSL, PH, PRH, UMH	64B
DAS NEUGEBO	Come, Holy [Ghost]	LCA, MSL, PH	09B
DENNIS	How Gentle God's Co	PH	31B, 33B
DEO GRACIAS	O Love, How [Deep]	NCH, PH, MSL, UMH	25B, 58B
DER LIEBEN	I Walk In Danger Al	MSL	58B
DEUS TUORUM	Take Up [Thy][Your]	MSL, NCH, PRH, UMH	21B, 54B
DIADEMATA	Make Me A Captive	LCA, PH, PRH, UMH	13B
"	Now In The Days Of	NCH, PH	33B
DICKINSON COL	Creator Spirit, Come	NCH	56B
DIVINUM MYS	Of The Father's Lov	LCA, MSL, PH, PRH, UMH	02B, 07B
"	Of The Parent's Hea	NCH	02B, 07B

DIX	As With Gladness	LCA, MSL, NCH, PH, PRH	10B
"	For The Beauty Of	LCA, NCH, PH, PRH, UMH	55B
"	Praise To God, Immo	PH	15B
DOMINUS REG	Such Perfect Love M	NCH	31B
"	The King Of Love My	LCA, MSL, PH, PRH, UMH	26B, 44B
DONNE SECOU	Father, In Thy Myst	PH	19B
"	Hope Of The World	MSL, PH	31B, 46B
DOWN AMPNEY	Come [Forth][Down]	LCA, MSL, NCH, PH, UMH	01B, 33B, 48B
DU MEINE SE	Lift Up Your Heart	PH	30B
DUKE STREET	Forth In [Thy][Your]	LCA, MSL, PH, UMH	45B
"	Jesus Shall Reign	LCA, MSL, NCH, PH, PRH, UMH	56B, 64B
DUNDEE	God Moves In A Myst	LCA, MSL, NCH, PH, PRH	16B, 41B, 61B
"	Since You Have, Too	WJOSS	66B
"	You Are The Way;	MSL, NCH	47B
DUNFERMLINE	Behold Us, Lord, A	PH, LCA	19B
DURROW	O God, Thou Art The	PH	10B

E

EASTER HYMN	Christ The Lord Is	LCA, MSL, NCH, PH, PRH, UMH	28B
EBENEZER	Come, O Spirit, D	NCH	36B
"	God Hath Spoken By	UMH	14B
"	O The Deep, Deep Lo	PRH	25B
"	Thy Strong Word	MSL	14B
EIN' FESTE	A Mighty Fortress	LCA, MSL, NCH, PH, PRH, UMH	12B, 42B, 65B
EISENACH	O Love Of God, How	PH	07B
ELLACOMBE	Hosanna, Loud Hosan	MSL, NCH, PH, PRH, UMH	25B
"	I Sing The Mighty P	NCH, PH	35B, 52B
"	My Heart Sings Out W	NCH	04B
"	We Hail You God's A	NCH	01B
"	We Limit Not The Tru	NCH, PH	40B
"	We Sing The Almight	MSL	35B, 52B
ELLERS	Take Up The Song	WJOSS	67B
ENDLESS SO	We Cannot Own The S	NCH	53B
ENERGY	We Give [Thee] [You]	LCA, MSL, PH, PRH	67B
ENTER, REJO	Enter, Rejoice, And	NCH	53B
ERIE	What A Friend We	LCA, NCH, PH, PRH	19B, 58B
ERMUNTRE DI	Break Forth, O Beau	LCA, NCH, PH, PRH, UMH	05B
ES IST DAS	Salvation Unto Us	MSL	65B
ES IST EIN'	How Lovely Is Your	NCH	16B
ES WOLLE GOTT	May God Embrace Us	MSL	46B

EUCHARISTI	Bread Of The W	LCA, NCH, PH, UMH	50B
EVENTIDE	Abide With Me	LCA, MSL, NCH, PH, UMH	51B

F

FAITHFULNES	Great Is [Your][Th	NCH, UMH	15B, 34B, 62B
FANG DEIN W	With The Lord Begi	MSL	48B
FENNVILLE	Out Of The Depths,	LCA, NCH, UMH	27B, 49B
FESTAL SONG	For All [Thy][Your	LCA, MSL	45B
"	O Savior, For The	NCH	45B, 66B
"	Rise Up, O Church O	PRH	11B
"	Rise Up, O Men Of G	LCA, PH, UMH	11B
FINLANDIA	Be [Calm][Still], M	LCA, MSL, NCH, PH, PRH, UMH	13B, 24B, 42B
"	We Would Be Buildin	NCH, PH	31B, 63B
FOREST GREE	Now Bless The God O	NCH	01B-04B, 38B, 65B
"	O Little Town Of Be	MSL	03B
FREU DICH S	Comfort, Comfort Th	MSL	02B, 03B

G

GALILEAN	Hark, The Voice Of	MSL	59B
GALILEE	Jesus Calls Us O'er	LCA, NCH, PH, PRH, UMH	59B
GARDEN	I Come To The Garden	NCH, PRH, UMH	28B
GARTAN	Love Came Down At C	LCA, MSL, NCH, UMH	07B, 12B
GAUDEAMUS	Come, You Faith	MSL	28B
GELOBT SEI	Good Christian [Fri	LCA, MSL, NCH, PH, PRH, UMH	30B
GERMANY	Take Up [Thy][Yo	NCH, PRH, UMH	21B, 54B
"	Where Cross The Cr	LCA, NCH, PH, UMH	18B, 56B
GLORIOUS IS	Glorious Is [Thy]	NCH, PRH	24B
GO TELL IT	Go Tell It On The M	MSL, NCH, PH, PRH, UMH	08B
GRACE CHURC	Fight The Good Figh	MSL	14B, 51B
GRAND ISLE	I Sing A Song Of Th	NCH, PH, UMH	14B
GREENLAND	Lift Up Your Hearts,	NCH, PH	30B
GREENSLEEVE	What Child Is This	LCA, MSL, NCH, PH, PRH, UMH	07B
GROSSER GOT	Holy God, We Praise	LCA, MSL, PH, NCH, UMH	37B, 59B
GUIDE MY FE	Guide My Feet	NCH	59B

H

HALAD	O God In Heaven	NCH, UMH	60B
HAMBURG	When I Survey The	LCA, NCH, PH, PRH, UMH	26B
HANKEY	I Love To Tell The	LCA, NCH, UMH	11B, 32B, 56B
HANOVER	O Worship The King	LCA, MSL, NCH, PH, PRH, UMH	64B

HANOVER	[Ye][You] Servants	LCA, NCH, PH, PRH, UMH	18B, 33B, 59B, 64B
HE LEADETH	He Leadeth Me	LCA, PH, PRH, UMH	14B, 44B
HEINLEIN	Forty Days And Fo	NCH, PH	20B
"	Lord Of Sorrows, L	WJOSS	66B
HELMSLEY	Lo, He Comes With	LCA, PRH, UMH	64B
HERE I AM,	Here I Am, Lord	UMH	10B
HESPERUS	O God Of Love, O	LCA, MSL, NCH, PH	55B
"	O Grant Us Light	NCH	23B
HIGH STREET	Christ Loves The C	UMH	22B
HIGHER GROU	Higher Ground	NCH, PRH	15B
"	I'm Pressing On The	NCH, PRH	15B
HILARITER	The Whole Bright Wo	PH	30B
HOLINESS	Take Time To Be Hol	PRH, TSH, UMH	38B
HOW GREAT	How Great Thou Art	PRH, UMH	67B
HUMMEL	God's Glory Is A W	PH	14B
HURSLEY	Dear Jesus, In Who	UMH	54B
"	Sun Of My Soul, O	MSL	54B
HYFRYDOL	Come, [O][Thou] Lo	LCA, MSL, NCH, PH, PRH, UMH	02B
"	God The Spirit, Gu	NCH, UMH	37B
"	Holy, Holy, God Of	LBL	37B
"	Lord Of Glory, You	MSL	51B
HYMN TO JOY	Joyful, Joyful We	LCA, NCH, PH, PRH, UMH	28B, 45B, 62B

I

I AM [THINE	I Am Thine [Yours]	NCH, PRH, UMH	10B, 27B, 57B
I WANT TO B	Lord, I Want To B	NCH, PH, UMH	12B, 43B, 52B
I'M GOIN' A	I'm Goin'a Sing Wh	UMH	36B
I'VE GOT A	I've Got A Feeling	NCH	39B
IDA	Christ Will Come Ag	NCH	63B
IN BABILONE	Hail, Thou Once De	LCA, MSL, UMH	30B
"	O How Glorious, Fu	NCH, PH	41B
"	Son Of God, Eternal	MSL	20B
"	There's A Wideness	LCA, NCH, PH, PRH	24B, 60B
IN DIR IST	In [Thee][You] Is Gl	MSL, UMH	45B
INNOCENTS	Christian, Rise An	NCH, PH	11B, 53B, 62B
INTEGER VIT	Father Almighty, B	NCH, PH	42B
INTERCESSOR	Children Of God	NCH	19B
"	O Brother Man, Fol	LCA, PH	19B
IRBY	Once In Royal Davi	LCA, MSL, NCH, PRH, UMH	01B, 10B
ITALIAN HY	Christ For The Worl	LCA, PH, UMH	11B, 32B
"	Come, [Now][O][Thou	LCA, MSL, NCH, PH, PRH, UMH	37B
IVERSON	Spirit Of The Livi	NCH, PRH	50B, 61B

J

JEFFERSON	God Our Author A	NCH	56B
JESU, MEIN	[Jesu][Jesus], Price	LCA, MSL, NCH, PH, PRH, UMH	33B, 46B
JESUS, MEI	Jesus Lives! The	MSL	29B
JESUS LOVES	Jesus Loves Me	NCH, PRH, UMH	57B
JOEL	Healing River Of	COC	58B
JONES	I Will Lift The Clou	NCH	23B, 43B
"	I Will Make The Dark	NCH	23B, 43B
JUDAS MACCA	Thine [Be][Is] The	LCA, NCH, PH, PRH, UMH	29B
JULION	You Are Called To	NCH	32B

K

KATHERINE	God Of Change And	NCH, UMH	39B
"	Many Gifts, One Spi	NCH, UMH	39B
KEDRON	Sunset To Sunrise	PH	23B
KINGSFOLD	How Could A God Who	COC	27B
"	O Master Workman Of	PH	15B, 31B
"	To Mock Your Reign,	UMH	27B
KREMSER	We Praise [Thee] [You]	LCA, MSL, NCH, PH, PRH	67B

L

LAKEWOOD	Forth In [Thy][Your]	MSL	10B
LANCASHIRE	Lead On Eternal Sov	NCH	22B
"	Lead On O King Eter	LCA, PH, PRH, UMH	22B
LAND OF RE	Lord, Who Throughout	NCH, PH, UMH	19B
LANGRAN	Here, O My Lord, I	LCA, MSL, PH, PRH, UMH	26B, 38B
"	Lead Us, O Father	PH	18B
LASST UNS	All Creatures Of Our	MSL, NCH, PH, PRH, UMH	37B
"	From All That Dwell	LCA, MSL, NCH, PH, UMH	28B
LATTIMER	This Little Light Of	NCH, UMH	18B, 32B
LAUDA ANIMA	God, Whose Love Is	UMH	46B
"	Praise, My Soul, Th	LCA, PH, PRH, UMH	29B
"	Praise With Joy The	NCH	29B
LAUDES DOMI	Let Every Christian	NCH	36B
"	When Morning Gilds	LCA, MSL, NCH, PH, PRH, UMH	08B
LEANING	Leaning On The Ever	NCH	13B
LEONI	Community Of Christ	NCH	35B, 61B
"	The God Of Abraham	LCA, MSL, NCH, PH, PRH, UMH	21B, 30B
LET US BREA	Let Us Break Bread	NCH, PH, PRH, UMH	26B
LET US HOPE	Let Us Hope When	NCH	15B, 20B, 21B
LIEBSTER JE	Word Of God, Come	UMH	38B
LIFT EVERY	Lift Every Voice	NCH, UMC	45B

213

LIGHTBEAMS	Many Are The Ligh	NCH	12B, 32B
LINSTEAD	Faithful God, You	COC	08B, 58B
LIVING GOD	Spirit Of The Living	NCH, PRH, UMH	36B
LLANFAIR	Jesus Christ Is Rise	LCA, MSL, NCH, PH	28B
"	Praise The Lord, His	PH	15B
LLANHERNE	Angels Holy, High A	PH	33B
LLANSANNAN	God Of Earth And Se	PH	09B
LOB GOTT	Let Me Be [Thine][Y	MSL	48B
LOBE DEN HE	Praise To The Lord	LCA, MSL, PH, PRH, UMH	44B
"	Sing Praise To God	LCA, MSL, NCH, PRH	44B
LORD, MAKE	Lord, Make Me More	NCH	09B, 50B
LORD OF THE	Lord Of The Dance	UMH	45B

M

MACHT HOCH	Lift Up Your Heads,	MSL	02B
MAGDALEN	My Hope Is Built On	LCA, MSL	22B, 57B
MANTON	Sovereign And Trans	NCH	23B
MARGARET	Thou Didst Leave	LCA, PH, PRH	19B
MARIAS LOVSÅNG	My Heart Sings Out	COC	04B
MARION	Rejoice, O Pilgri	MSL	51B
"	Rejoice, [Ye][You	LCA, NCH, PH, UMH	51B
MARSH CHAPEL	Behold A Broken Worl	UMH	34B, 52B, 63B
MARTIN	Be Not Dismayed	NCH, PRH, UMH	39B, 62B, 67B
"	God Will Take Care	NCH, PRH, UMH	39B, 62B, 67B
MARTYRDOM	According To Thy Gr	LCA, PH, PRH	26B
"	As Pants The Hart F	LCA, NCH, PH	43B
"	As The Hart Longs	PRH	43B
MARY'S CHILD	Born In The Night, M	NCH	04B, 07B
MARYTON	O [Master][Savior]	LCA, NCH, PH, PRH, UMH	18B
MAUNDY THU	Christ At Table T	NCH	38B
McKEE	In Christ There Is	NCH, PH, PRH, UMH	31B, 53B
MEIN LEBEN	God Is My Strong Sal	PH	12B, 51B
MEIRIONYDID	The Voice Of God Is	PH, UMH	34B, 40B
MELITA	My Hope Is Built	LCA, MSL, PRH, UMH	22B, 34B, 57B
MESSAGE	We've A Story To Te	PRH, UMH	34B
MESSIAH	Take My Life And Le	LCA, MSL, NCH, PH, PRH, UMH	41B, 48B, 52B
MICHAEL	All My Hope Is Firm	UMH	34B, 57B
"	All My Hope On God	NCH	34B
MILWAUKEE	Lift Up Your Heads,	MSL	02B
MIT FREU	Sing Praise To God	NCH, PH, UMH	44B
MITTEN WIR	In The Very Midst	MSL	49B, 57B
MONKS GATE	All Who Would Valia	MSL	10B, 47B
MONSELL	Worship The Lord In	PH, PRH	55B
MOODY	Grace Greater Than	PRH, UMH	22B
MORECAMBE	Here, O My Lord, I	LCA, MSL, NCH, PH, PRH, UMH	38B

214

MORECAMBE	Spirit Of God Desce	LCA, NCH, PH, PRH, UMH	36B
MORNING HYM	Forth In [Thy][Your	LCA, PH, UMH	10B
MORNING SON	As Moses Raised The	NCH	23B
MORNING STA	Brightest And Best	LCA, MSL, NCH, PH	08B
MORNINGTON	Teach Me, My God	LCA, PH	24B, 25B, 62B
MURRAY	Come, Teach Us, Spi	NCH	25B, 48B
MY TRIBUTE	How Can I Say Thanks	MSL, NCH, PRH	29B, 54B

N

NATIONAL HY	God Of Our Fathers	LCA, MSL, PH, PRH	46B
"	God Of The Ages, Wh	NCH, UMH	46B
NEAR THE CR	Jesus, Keep Me Nea	NCH, PRH, UMH	22B
NEED	I Need [Thee][You]	LCA, NCH, PH, PRH, UMH	42B, 60B
NEED OF PR	Not My Brother, Nor	NCH	56B
"	Standing In The Nee	NCH	56B
NETTLETON	Come, O Fount of Ev	NCH, UMH	47B
"	Holy Spirit, Ever D	NCH	49B
NEUMARK	If [You][Thou] But	LCA, MSL, NCH, PH, UMH	15B, 39B, 61B
NEW BEGINNI	We Plant A Grain Of	NCH	41B
NEW DIMENSI	In The Midst Of New	NCH	20B, 49B, 57B
NEW HOPE	Jesus Took The Brea	NCH	38B
NEW SONG	You Gave My Heart	COC	30B, 44B
NICAEA	Holy, Holy, Holy	LCA, MSL, NCH, PH, PRH, UMH	29B, 37B, 59B
NORRIS	Where He Leads Me	UMH	40B
NUN DANKET	Now Thank We All	LCA, MSL, NCH, PH, PRH, UMH	16B, 51B, 65B
NUN FREUT	O God Of All Your	NCH	51B
NUN KOMM, D	Savior Of The Nation	MSL, UMH	04B
NUN LAST UN	"Take Up Your Cross,	MSL	21B, 54B
NUN LOB, ME	I Know My Faith Is	MSL	57B, 65B

O

O DASS ICH	By Grace I'm Saved	MSL	65B
O FILII ET	O Sons And Daughter	COC, LCA, MSL, NCH, PH, UMH	28B
O GOD, MY GO	O God, My God	NCH	58B
O GOTT, DU	How Can I Thank You,	MSL	29B
O GROSSER G	O God Of God, O Lig	MSL	55B
O JESU	I Look To [Thee][Yo	LCA, NCH, PRH, PH	58B
O QUANTA QU	O What Their Joy And	LCA, NCH, PH, UMH	66B
O WALY WALY	When Love Is Found	NCH, UMH	57B
OBERLIN	He Came As Grace	GG	01B
OGONTZ	By Whatever Name	NCH	59B
OLD 124TH	God Of The Prophets	MSL	18B
OLD 22ND	Thou God Of All, Wh	PH	53B
"	We Limit Not The Tr	NCH, PH	40B

OLD HUNDR	All People That On	LCA, MSL, NCH, PH, PRH, UMH	48B
"	Before Jehovah's A	MSL	10B, 51B
"	From All That Dwell	LCA, MSL, PH, UMH	28B
OLIVET	My Faith Looks Up	LCA, MSL, PH, PRH, UMH	57B
"	Sorrow And Grief Ha	WJOSS	66B
OMNI DIE	For The Faithful Wh	NCH	35B, 62B
OPEN MY E	Open My Eyes	UMH, PRH	34B, 54B

P

PARK STREE	Before Jehovah's A	LCA, PH	51B
PASS ME NOT	Pass Me Not, O Gent	LCA, NCH, PRH, UMH	53B
PASSION CHO	O God, How We Have	NCH	20B
"	We Yearn, O [Chris	GG, NCH	01B
PATMOS	Take My Life, O Lor	MSL	48B, 52B
PEACE LIKE	I've Got Peace L	NCH, PRH	42B
PEACE, MY	Peace I Leave Wi	NCH	46B
PEEK	I Would Be True	NCH, PH	21B, 62B
PENITENT	It's Me, It's Me, O	UMH	56B
"	Not My Brother, Nor	UMH	56B
PENITENTIA	Here, O My Lord, I	UMH	38B
PENTECOST	Every Time I Feel T	NCH, UMH	37B
"	Fight The Good Figh	LCA, PH	14B, 51B
"	Let There Be Light	PH, NCH	18B
PICARDY	Let All Mortal Fles	LCA, MSL, NCH, PH, UMH	03B, 38B
"	Lo, He Comes With C	MSL	64B
PILOT	Jesus, Savior, Pilo	LCA, MSL, NCH, PH, UMH	42B
PLEADING SAVI	Lord, We Thank Thee	PH	32B
"	Thank Our God For Sis	NCH	32B
PORT JERVIS	We Are The Church	UMH	40B
PRECIOUS LO	Precious Lord, Take	NCH, PRH, UMH	43B
PROCESSION	Praise The Source	NCH	50B
PROMISE	In The Bulb There I	NCH	47B
"	Hymn Of Promise	UMH	47B
PROMISES	Standing On The Pro	PRH, UMH	60B
PSALM 42	Comfort, Comfort [O	LCA, NCH, PH	02B, 03B
PUER NOBIS	Creator Spirit, Come	NCH	56B
"	Joy Dawned Again On	NCH, PH	29B
"	O Holy Spirit, Roo	NCH	49B
"	Unto Us A Boy Is Bor	PH	05B

Q

QUEM PASTOR	Grant Us Wisdom To	NCH	50B

R

RAQUEL	Hear The Voice Of G	NCH	60B
RATHBUN	In The Cross Of Ch	LCA, MSL, NCH, PH, PRH UMH	23B

REGENSBURG	Father, Hear The Pr	PH	14B, 18B
REGENT SQUA	Lord, Dismiss Us Wi	MSL	08B, 37B
REPTON	Return, My People	NCH	04B, 19B
RESCUE	Rescue The Perishin	PRH, UMH	16B
Response	Into My Heart, Lord	TSH	09B, 41B, 52B
REST	Dear God, Embracing	NCH	47B
"	Dear Lord And Fathe	LCA, PH, PRH, UMH	47B
REUTER	God's Word Is Our G	LCA, MSL	65B
RHOSYMEDRE	My Song Is Love Unk	LCA, MSL, NCH, PH	24B
"	O God, Whose Steadf	NCH	55B
"	Our Father, By Whos	MSL, PH	55B
RICHMOND	O For A Heart To Pr	LCA, PRH, UMH	59B
RIVER FORES	As Moses, Lost In S	MSL	23B
ROBINSON	Give Thanks For Lif	NCH	66B
ROCKING	Little Jesus, Sweet	PH	05B
"	Rock-a-Bye, My Dear	UMH	05B
ROCKINGHAM	Incarnate God, Imm	NCH	41B
"	Strong Son Of God,	PH	41B
"	Teach Me, My God	LCA	24B, 25B, 62B
"	Teach Me, O Lord,	NCH	24B, 25B, 62B
"	Teach Me Thy Way,	PRH	24B, 25B
" OLD	When I Survey The	MSL	26B
ROEDER	God Of The Sparrow,	NCH, UMH	27B
ROLLINGBAY	May The Sending One	NCH	39B
RUSSIAN HYM	God The Omnipotent	LCA, NCH, PH, PRH	11B, 22B
RUTH	When Mary Bathed O	COC	26B

S

SAFETY	Love Lifted Me	PRH, TSH	23B
ST. AGNES	Come, Holy Spirit,	NCH, PH, PRH	50B
ST. ANDREW	Jesus Calls Us O'er	LCA, NCH, PH	09B
ST. ANNE	[O][Our] God, Our He	LCA, MSL, NCH, PH, UMH	24B, 45B
ST. BREND	We Are One In The	PRH	35B
ST. BRIDE	Give To The Winds T	PH, UMH	11B
"	Out Of The Depths I	LCA, NCH, UMH	27B
ST. CATHERI	Faith Of Our Father	LCA, PH, PRH, UMH	11B
"	Faith Of The Martyr	NCH	11B
ST. CHRISTO	Before [The][Your]	NCH, PH	21B, 54B
"	Beneath The Cross O	LCA, NCH, PH, PRH, UMH	27B
ST. COLUMBA	The King Of Love My	LCA, MSL, PH, PRH, UMH	26B, 44B
ST. DENIO	God Made From One B	NCH	18B, 55B
"	Immortal, Invisible	LCA, MSL, NCH, PH, PRH, UMH	16B, 62B
ST. DROSTAN	Ride On, Ride On In	LCA, MSL, NCH, PH	25B
ST. DUNSTAN	[All][He] Who Would	LCA, NCH, PH	10B, 47B
ST. FLAVIAN	Be Known To Us In	NCH, PH	38B
"	Lord Jesus, Who Thr	NCH	20B
"	When Mary Bathed O	COC	26B
"	Where Charity And L	NCH	31B

ST. GEORGE'S	Come, [O] [Ye] Than	LCA, MSL, NCH, PH, PRH, UMH	67B
ST. GERTRUD	Forward Through The	NCH, PH, UMH	41B
ST. HILDA	O Jesus, Thou Art St	LCA, PH	19B
ST. KEVIN	Come, O Spirit, Wit	NCH, PRH	36B
"	Come, [Ye][You] Fai	LCA, NCH, PH, UMH	28B
"	God Of Wisdom, God	COC	51B
ST. LOUIS	O Little Town Of Be	LCA, MSL, NCH, PH, PRH, UMH	03B
ST. MAGNUS	The Head That Once	LCA, PH	35B
ST. MICHAEL	In Everything Give T	WJOSS	67B
"	O Come And Dwell	UMH	36B
"	O Day Of God, Draw	NCH, PH, UMH	11B, 64B
"	Send Down Thy Truth	PH	09B
ST. PETER	In Christ There Is	NCH, PH	31B, 53B
"	Where Charity And L	NCH, UMH	26B, 31B, 63B
ST. PETERSB	I Sing The Praise Of	NCH	39B
ST. THEODUL	All Glory, Laud, An	LCA, MSL, NCH, PH, PRH, UMH	25B
"	O How Shall I Recei	NCH	01B
ST. THOMAS	I Love [Thy][Your]	MSL, NCH, PH, UMH	56B
SAKURA	Praise To God	NCH	28B, 52B
SALZBURG	Let The Whole Creati	LCA, PH	33B
SANDON	God Of Our Life, Th	NCH, PH	16B, 35B, 60B
"	Unto The Hills We L	NCH	25B
SCARLET RI	Who Would Think Tha	NCH	08B
SCHMÜCKE D	Deck Thyself, My So	UMH	50B
"	Deck Thyself With G	LCA	50B
"	Graced With Garment	NCH	50B
"	Soul, Adorn Yoursel	MSL	50B
SCHÖNSTER	Beautiful [Jesus][Sa	LCA, MSL, NCH	24B
"	Fairest Lord Jesus	PH, PRH, UMH	24B
SEDONA	All Earth Is Waiting	GG	02B
SEELENBRÄU	Jesus, Still Lead On	LCA, MSL, NCH	45B
SERENITY	Immortal Love, Fore	NCH, PH	08B, 13B, 46B
SERVANT SON	Won't You Let Me Be	NCH	61B
SHARPTHORNE	What Does The Lord	PRH, UMH	47B
SHEPHERDS'	Deep In The Shadows	NCH	19B
"	The Lord Is Rich	PH	19B
SHOW ALTER	Leaning On The Ever	PRH, UMH	13B
SICILIAN MA	Lord, Dismiss Us W	LCA, NCH, PH, PRH, UMH	08B, 37B
SINE NOMIN	For All The Saint	LCA, MSL, NCH, PH, PRH, UMH	66B
SLANE	Be [Now][Thou] My	NCH, PH, PRH, UMH	11B, 50B
"	Christ Be My Leader	MSL	11B, 50B
SOLID ROCK	My Hope Is Built On	NCH, PRH	22B, 34B, 57B
SONG 13	Holy Spirit, Light	MSL	51B
SONG OF RE	Strengthen All The	NCH	21B, 64B
SOUL SHEPH	Shepherd Of My Soul	COC	30B

SOUTHWELL	Have Faith In God,	PH, PRH	44B, 48B
"	Lord Jesus, Think On	MSL	44B
SPARROW	God's Eye Is On The	NCH	15B
SPIRIT	Spirit, Spirit Of G	NCH	14B, 31B
STEAL AWAY	Steal Away	NCH, UMH	39B
STILLE NACH	Silent Night	LCA, MSL, NCH, PH, PRH, UMH	05B
STOOKEY	O The Depth Of Love	UMH	50B
STORIES O	Tell Me the [Story]	PRH, TSH, UMH	25B, 43B
STUTTGART	Come, [O]] [Thou] Lo	LCA, NCH, PH, UMH	03B
"	O My Soul, Bless	NCH, PH	44B
SURSUM CORD	How Like A Gentle S	NCH, UMH	42B, 62B
SWEET HOUR	Sweet Hour Of Praye	NCH, PH, PRH, UMH	63B

T

TAFT STREET	We Thank You God	COC	48B
TALAVERA TER	Take My [Gifts][Life	LCA, NCH, PRH	41B, 67B
TALITHA CUM	There Was Jesus By	NCH	43B
TALLIS' T	How Could A God Who	COC	27B
"	How Deep The Silenc	NCH	42B, 60B
TAULÉ	All Earth Is Waitin	NCH, UMH	02B
TENDERNESS	Sacred The Body	COC	32B
"	Touch The Earth Lig	NCH	55B
TERRA BEATA	God Reigns O'er All	NCH	24B, 48B
"	This Is My Father's	LCA, PH, PRH, UMH	24B, 48B
THE ASHGROVE	Sent Forth By God's	MSL, UMH	45B
THE FIRST N	The First Nowell	LCA, NCH, PH, UMH	02B
THE KING'S	Ride On, Ride On In	MSL	25B
THE OLD RUG	On A Hill Far Away	NCH, PRH, UMH	22B
THE SOLID R	My Hope Is Built	LCA, NCH, PRH, UMH	22B, 34B, 57B
THIRD MODE	I Heard The Voice O	LCA, MSL, NCH, PRH	60B
THY WORD	Thy Word Is A Lamp	PH, UMH	38B
TOA-SIA	God Created Heaven	NCH, UMH	09B
TOULON	God Of The Prophets	NCH, PH	18B
TRENTHAM	Breathe On Me, Brea	LCA, NCH, PH, PRH, UMH	09B, 43B
TRURO	Christ Is Alive	UMH	30B
"	Lift Up Your Heads,	LCA, NCH, PH, UMH	02B
TRUST AND O	Trust And Obey	PRH, UMH	40B, 59B
TRUST IN JE	'Tis So Sweet To	PRH, UMH	57B
TRUST IN THE L	I Will Trust In The L	NCH, UMH	61B
TRYGGARE K	Children Of The Hea	LCA, PRH, UMH	44B

U

UFFINGHAM	Creator Of The Eart	UMH	20B
"	Lord, Save Thy Worl	PH	20B
UNION SEMIN	Draw Us In The Spir	NCH, UMH	63B
Unknown	Give Of Your Best T	TSH	14B

V

VATER UNSER	Jesus, [Thy][Your]	LCA, MSL	58B
"	Our Father, Who Fro	MSL	56B
VENI EMMANU	[O] [Oh] Come, O	LCA, MSL, NCH, PH, PRH, UMH	01B
VICAR	Hope Of The World	PH, UMH	55B
VICTORY	The Strife Is O'er	LCA, NCH, PH, UMH	29B
VIENNA	Jesus, With Thy Ch	LCA, NCH, PH	53B
"	Take My Life And Le	LCA, MSL, PH, PRH	09B, 41B
VIETNAM	My Prayer Rises To	UMH	52B
VOM HIMMEL	A Child Is Born	LBL	03B

W

WACHET AUF	Keep Awake, Be Alwa	NCH	03B
"	Wake, Awake, For Nig	LCA, MSL, NCH, PH, UMH	03B
WAS MEIN G	Who Trusts In God,	MSL, PH	46B
WE SHALL O	We Shall Overcome	NCH	27B
WE TRUST IN	When The Winds Rage	COC	58B
WEBB	Now Is The Time App	NCH	16B, 53B
"	Remember God Was Gu	GG	35B
"	Stand Up, Stand Up	LCA, MSL, PH, PRH, UMH	35B
WEISSE FLAG	Son Of God, Eternal	LCA, PH	20B
WELLESLEY	There's A Wideness	PH, UMH	54B
WELLSPRING	Wellspring Of Wisdom	UMH	13B
WELWYN	Children Of God	NCH	19B, 55B
"	O Brother Man, Fol	LCA, PH	19B, 55B
WENN WIR IN	When In The Hour Of	MSL	60B
WER NUR D	I Leave All Things	MSL	63B
"	If [You][Thou] But	LCA, MSL, NCH, PH, UMH	47B
WESTMINSTER	For The Healing Of	NCH, UMH	22B
WEXFORD CAR	A Woman Came Who	NCH	25B
WHEN JESUS	When Jesus Wept	NCH	20B
WHITFIELD	We Are [God's][Your	MSL, NCH, PRH	61B
WHITNEY	Love Came Down At	LCA, NCH, UMH	07B, 12B
WIE SCHÖN	O Holy Spirit, Ente	LCA, MSL, PH	48B
WILD MOUNT	Spirit, Open My Hear	COC	49B
WINCHSTR N	Before Jehovah's Aw	LCA, PH	10B
"	On [River] Jordan's	LCA, MSL, NCH, PH	03B
"	Ride On! Ride On In	LCA, NCH, PH	25B
WINCHE OLD	Behold Us, Lord A	LCA, PH	19B
"	While Shepherds Watc	LCA, MSL, PH, PRH, UMH	07B
"	You Gave My Heart	COC	30B, 44B
WINSTON-SAL	O God, As With A Pot	NCH	39B
WITTENBERG	O God, O Lord Of Hea	MSL	54B
WIR GLAUB	We All Believe In On	MSL, PH	37B
WIR PFLÜGEN	We [Plough][Plow]	LCA, PH	52B
WOLFE	Surely The Presence	UMH	36B

WONDROUS L	What Wondrous Love	NCH, UMH	27B
WOODLANDS	Tell Out, My Soul	PRH, UMH	03B, 12B
WOODWORTH	Just As I Am	LCA, MSL, NCH, PH,	
		PRH, UMH	20B, 54B
WORKING	God Is At Work In	COC	44B
WUNDERBARE	God Himself Is Pre	LCA, MSL, PH	33B
"	God Is Truly With	NCH	33B

Y

YARNTON	We Are Not Our Own	NCH	41B
YATTENDON 46	We Give [Thee] [You]	LCA, MSL, PH, PRH	67B
YIGDAL	The God Of Abraham	LCA, MSL, NCH, PH	
		PRH, UMH	21B, 30B
YORKSHIRE	Christians, Awake,	LCA, PH	05B
"	Rejoice, O People,	PH	40B

Z

ZION	Guide Me, O My Gre	NCH	21B

221

Lectionary Preaching After Pentecost

The following index will aid the user of this book in matching the correct Sunday with the appropriate text during Pentecost. During the Pentecost season, this book lists Sundays by Proper (following the Revised Common and Episcopal lectionary system). Lutheran and Roman Catholic designations indicate days comparable to Sundays on which the Propers are used.

(Fixed dates do not pertain to Lutheran Lectionary)

Fixed Date Lectionaries *Revised Common (including ELCA)* *and Roman Catholic*	Lutheran Lectionary *Lutheran*
The Day of Pentecost	The Day of Pentecost
The Holy Trinity	The Holy Trinity
May 29-June 4 — Proper 4, Ordinary Time 9	Pentecost 2
June 5-11 — Proper 5, Ordinary Time 10	Pentecost 3
June 12-18 — Proper 6, Ordinary Time 11	Pentecost 4
June 19-25 — Proper 7, Ordinary Time 12	Pentecost 5
June 26-July 2 — Proper 8, Ordinary Time 13	Pentecost 6
July 3-9 — Proper 9, Ordinary Time 14	Pentecost 7
July 10-16 — Proper 10, Ordinary Time 15	Pentecost 8
July 17-23 — Proper 11, Ordinary Time 16	Pentecost 9
July 24-30 — Proper 12, Ordinary Time 17	Pentecost 10
July 31-Aug. 6 — Proper 13, Ordinary Time 18	Pentecost 11
Aug. 7-13 — Proper 14, Ordinary Time 19	Pentecost 12
Aug. 14-20 — Proper 15, Ordinary Time 20	Pentecost 13
Aug. 21-27 — Proper 16, Ordinary Time 21	Pentecost 14
Aug. 28-Sept. 3 — Proper 17, Ordinary Time 22	Pentecost 15
Sept. 4-10 — Proper 18, Ordinary Time 23	Pentecost 16
Sept. 11-17 — Proper 19, Ordinary Time 24	Pentecost 17
Sept. 18-24 — Proper 20, Ordinary Time 25	Pentecost 18
Sept. 25-Oct. 1 — Proper 21, Ordinary Time 26	Pentecost 19
Oct. 2-8 — Proper 22, Ordinary Time 27	Pentecost 20

Oct. 9-15 — Proper 23, Ordinary Time 28	Pentecost 21
Oct. 16-22 — Proper 24, Ordinary Time 29	Pentecost 22
Oct. 23-29 — Proper 25, Ordinary Time 30	Pentecost 23
Oct. 30-Nov. 5 — Proper 26, Ordinary Time 31	Pentecost 24
Nov. 6-12 — Proper 27, Ordinary Time 32	Pentecost 25
Nov. 13-19 — Proper 28, Ordinary Time 33	Pentecost 26
	Pentecost 27
Nov. 20-26 — Christ the King	Christ the King

Reformation Day (or last Sunday in October) is October 31 (Revised Common, Lutheran)

All Saints' Day (or first Sunday in November) is November 1 (Revised Common, Lutheran, Roman Catholic)